Lysa is able to balance her spiritual pursuits and not forget the reality of being a wife and mom. She offers a fresh approach to setting goals and purposes to one's life. Her lifetime experience adds humor and realism to this book. The reader will be encouraged as she reads this book.

EMILIE BARNES, *Author, Speaker*

With humor and solid advice, Lysa helps us find balance and sanity in this crazy wonderful world of womanhood.

BECKY FREEMAN, *Author, Speaker*

As women, we are called to serve the Lord and others by finding our purpose. Lysa's book and journal will release women from the frustration of not having a plan or a track to run on. Lysa herself went from a life that lacked purpose and direction to one of fulfilling a purpose. She went from unorganized to organized, from frustration to enjoyment in the most precious aspects of life—that of a homemaker, wife, mother, and head of The Proverbs 31 Ministry. I highly recommend this book to women of all ages.

SALLY MEREDITH, *Co-author of* Two Becoming One
Vice President of Christian Family Life

Living Life on Purpose

DISCOVERING GOD'S BEST FOR YOUR LIFE

Lysa TerKeurst

All Scripture quotations, unless otherwise indicated, are taken from the *Holy Bible, New International Version*®. NIV®. Copyright © 1973, 1978, 1984 by International Bible Society. Used by permission of Zondervan Publishing House. All rights reserved.

Scripture quotations marked NASB are taken from the *NEW AMERICAN STANDARD BIBLE*®, © Copyright The Lockman Foundation 1960, 1962, 1963, 1968, 1971, 1972, 1973, 1975, 1977, 1995. Used by permission. (www.Lockman.org)

Scripture quotations marked TLB are taken from *The Living Bible* copyright © 1971. Used by permission of Tyndale House Publishers, Inc., Wheaton, Illinois 60189. All rights reserved.

Scripture quotations marked NKJV are taken from the *New King James Version*. Copyright © 1982 by Thomas Nelson, Inc. Used by permission. All rights reserved.

Scripture quotations marked KJV are taken from the King James Version.

Library of Congress Cataloging-in-Publication Data

TerKeurst, Lysa
    Living life on purpose: discovering God's best for your life / Lysa TerKeurst
        p. cm.
    Includes bibliographical references.
    ISBN 0-8024-4195-5
    1. Christian women—Religious life. I. Title.
BV4527 .T46 2000

                                                    248.8'.43—dc21

1 3 5 7 9 10 8 6 4 2

Printed in the United States of America

CONTENTS

ACKNOWLEDGMENTS

A special thank you goes to:

Scott and Elaine Mayson, who first introduced me to the concept of having a Life Plan and who live lives worth modeling.

My mom, who believed in me when I didn't believe in myself. You put wings to my dreams. How can I ever thank you for your encouragement, support, and love?

My special mom through marriage. Thanks for raising such an amazing son, for supporting me, and loving the girls.

My sweet sisters, Angee, Sarah, Emily, Monica, and Ann Marie, who helped me with my girls, sent great stories and quotes via E-mail, and encouraged me that I had a message worth sharing.

My partner and friend, Sharon Jaynes. Thank you for holding me up when I get weary, cheering me on in victory, walking with me hand-in-hand in ministry, and mostly for being my friend. Thank you, also, for helping pen the Seven Principles of the Proverbs 31 Woman, on which so much of this book is founded.

My kindred spirit, Cheri Jimenez. Thank you for helping to pen the Seven Principles and for your willingness to sacrificially serve The Proverbs 31 Ministry. You helped carry the ministry so that it could be possible for me to write this book. Thank you, also, for your never-tiring ear and your encouraging words as I read and reread sections of this manuscript.

My eating, sleeping, and breathing-the-Word-of-God friend, Sheila Mangum. Your wisdom in developing the Bible study portion of the journal was invaluable! I can't wait to see you dance down the streets of gold with your "Daddy."

My you-can-do-it friends: Glynnis Whitwer, Genia Rogers, Lori

Willis, Renee Marston, Tracy Roberts, Linda Beerbower, Laura Kasay, Suzy Sandbo, and Renée Swope. Thank you for your advice, honesty, prayers, and encouragement.

A special thank-you to Lynn Pitts and Jan Harrison—you have been so kind to me—and to Wade Pearce for keeping me on my toes.

My small group: David and Becky, Scott and Melanie, Mark and Heidi, Jeff and Gina, and Jimmy and Alli. You prayed this book into existence and helped out in so many ways.

My special helpers: Andrea, Samantha, and Alicia Driver—also, Sarah Joyner and Chapel Cromer. You have all been a blessing from God! (Renee, Pam, and Cass—you are great moms!)

The special "Golds" Bible Study Group. Thank you for being the first group to walk through this book. While you all kept thanking me for teaching you, I must admit I learned as much from you. May you each embrace God's love for you and continue to seek Him with all your heart.

The entire team at Moody: Greg Thornton, especially, for catching the vision and recognizing God's timing; Kelly Cluff for encouraging me to send in the proposal; Julie Ieron for coaching me, encouraging me, and never letting me settle for second best; Anne Scherich for combing through the manuscript with a fine-tooth comb and getting all the tangles out.

To all the women who want to find purpose for their lives: God is about to take you on quite a journey. May you discover joy, peace, and hope for an amazing future.

$\mathcal{I}$NTRODUCTION

$\mathcal{I}$ feel it's only fair that I tell you a few things before you read this book. If you are looking to read a book written by someone who has mastered this thing called life, you might be disappointed. If you are seeking marital wisdom, you might not like the fact that I have raised my voice beyond an acceptable decibel level a time or two. If a woman whose children daily rise and call her blessed is what you want, please don't call my home before 8:00 A.M. on a school morning. My children might call me something but it probably would not be blessed. I've been known to try to improvise using lip liner as eyeliner, not realizing that red and brown are not as close as I would have liked on the color chart. Then I couldn't get the mess off and had to walk around with red clown eyes for three days. My house isn't always perfectly clean, my accounts aren't always balanced, and chocolate is a major weakness during most dieting attempts.

I struggle at times, just like you. But I have found that by doing the things I write about in this book, life has become more meaningful, manageable, and enjoyable. I want to always be on a continual journey toward discovering God's best for my life. Living my life "on purpose" is something I believe honors God and gives me peace. I know that I am doing what He created me to do. Knowing this adds a dimension of value to everything I do, which was a missing link in my life for so very long. God has taken me on quite an adventure to teach me these insights. Let me give you a glimpse of my life before I had a life plan.

Ten years ago I could have been voted "Least Likely to Ever Write a Book on Living Life on Purpose." I was a schedule rebel who thought planning was for people who had no desire for excitement in their dull, well-organized lives. Well, God has such a sense of humor! He had plans for my life that I could never have imagined. When I was single, I knew I needed to get a better handle on balancing my life but decided that

I'd put it off until I was married. Then I got married and decided to put it off until I had children. By the time our first child arrived I was totally overwhelmed. All I could see was a disorganized home, a struggling marriage, an overweight body, and a baby who didn't like to sleep. I started praying that God would bring other women into my life so maybe I could learn from their experiences. It wasn't long before God answered my prayers and a friend asked me to join her in writing a newsletter based on Proverbs 31. *Great,* I thought, *I love to write, and I'll get to meet other women. This is just what I've been praying for.* Then I went home and read Proverbs 31.

My response then became less than enthusiastic. "Excuse me, God, I know you've never been known to make a mistake, but this time you seem to have forgotten a few of the qualities that you and I know about me. You are asking the woman who not only doesn't know how to make coverings for beds but went almost a year not knowing she was supposed to wash her sheets. And, about this issue of considering a field before she buys it . . . well, that's just not me at all. I charge (literally) full steam ahead, and if that card gets rejected I'll just write a check. I figure as long as I have checks in my checkbook I must have money in my account. Then there's the thing where her children rise up and call her blessed and her husband praises her. Well, I don't mean to question you, God, but my family does not always sing my praises, and the last time I rode by the city gates I was speeding and honking so loudly I must have missed that awards ceremony they were holding to praise my works!"

Well, after I got through with my little tantrum, the Lord posed an important question. "Are you through? Good, because now I can begin." The Lord had wonderful plans to shape me, mold me, and, yes, use me for his glory. I couldn't see past the dirt on the kitchen floor.

Then I found out we were expecting again. There I sat with a six-month-old on my lap, another positive pregnancy test in my hand, and a deadline I needed to meet for the *Proverbs 31 Woman* newsletter. I was supposed to write an article to encourage wives and mothers. The article would definitely have to wait. I glanced out the window to see my husband barreling down the driveway. They let him out on good behavior; what could *I* do to get pardoned? I picked up the baby and made my way to the kitchen, only to trip over the baby swing, which triggered a flood of tears from us both. The house was a wreck and so was I. Not only did I not know how to bring order to all of this, I didn't even know where to get started. I peered out the window again. Wasn't there a super-hero out there somewhere who was supposed to rescue us damsels in distress? Suddenly, there was a knock on the door. Could it be? Was it a bird? A plane? No, it was my very angry neighbor informing me that my dog had been an uninvited guest at her outdoor party yesterday. He ate her ham and dragged her roast off into the woods.

I called my husband and asked him how much longer it would be before he could come home, only to have him remind me he'd only been gone thirty minutes. Through my tears I recounted the neighbor's story for him. He suggested that we take the dog to the pound, since this was her third and probably final strike with the neighbors. I wondered if there was a "people pound" where strays like me could go to get adopted into better situations. Art suggested I get out of the house and maybe go to an aerobics class or something.

After hanging up in disgust, I thought, "Wow, that sure would be a pretty sight. What would those stick figures think of me?" I decided to crawl back in bed. Maybe if I dreamed about exercise, I could lose a pound or two. I needed help. I needed direction. I needed a plan.

I could remember feeling this desperate another time in my life. It was my junior year in college and I was failing economics. I called my dad and asked him if he could please call the dean of the business school and make a plea on my behalf to let me drop the class. He said that he would not call the dean. I started crying, and he tried to comfort me by recounting his experience in a class he had almost failed. The university now invites him back to teach that very class. We ended the conversation with me assuring him I never wanted to teach economics. A few days later I got a letter in the mail from my dad. Part of it read, "Do your best in life but keep life in perspective. Your mom and I are proud of you for not quitting even though that would be the easiest thing to do."

Dad's wisdom and words of encouragement never left me. Just like I'd done in that economics class many years before, I determined not to quit and decided to seek out help. I decided to start with the most organized and together person I knew, my husband.

Art was more than happy to research possible solutions to my dilemma. A friend from work introduced him to a life plan concept that he and his wife had found to be very beneficial. Art knew this was the answer. He came home and told me all about this exciting planning adventure that he wanted us to go on. The whole idea sounded pointless and totally boring to me, but because I was desperate, I agreed. We went away for what I thought was a waste of a perfectly good weekend and returned changed people.

For the first time in our marriage we shared dreams about our future and realized that in order to make them a reality, we needed a plan. We needed our own individual life plans as well as a corporate plan for our family. So we became a team, working together toward common goals in every area of life. We developed a budget, established family nights and date nights, and started planning dream vacations. We set goals for every area of our lives from physical to financial. We decided to take time on Sunday afternoons for our weekly evaluation planning sessions to discuss plans for that particular week and schedule our date night and family night. We saw wonderful benefits for our family from having a Life Plan. This was the starting point for getting my life together. I had a newfound purpose and plans to live each day intentionally. I had goals to shoot for and rewards to look forward to for each goal that I met. Larger projects were broken down into smaller more manageable jobs. My life became more organized and happy as a result of establishing a plan. Did I stick to it perfectly? No. Was it instrumental in changing my life? Most definitely!

Now, back to why I'm writing this book. You see, God chose to use an imperfect, scatterbrained person to be the vessel through which to send this message forth because it would insure Him all the credit. Also, it would encourage others to know that if God could do this with me, He can certainly do this with them.

I have learned a great deal about the importance of planning and bringing a sense of order to my life thus enabling *me* to "live life on purpose"! I now know that the Proverbs 31 woman did not accomplish all she did in one day. No, it took a lifetime of living her life on purpose to get to the place we find her. Her life should challenge us and give us an example to follow, not something to intimidate us. After I got past this intimidation, I decided that I liked this Proverbs 31 woman and the way she lived. I liked how her life turned out, with her husband praising her and her children rising to call her blessed. I liked that she worked hard and was respected for all she did. I liked that she was well prepared and that she smiled at the days to come.

Over the years I have continued to improve, update, and revise my plan. My Life Plan has now become more than just a way to help me get a better handle on my schedule. It has now become my account of a life well lived. Using God-inspired life statements as my guide, I can now answer the fundamental questions of life. I am fulfilling my purpose in each of the major areas of my life. I have a well thought-out and prayed-through plan to help me become a Proverbs 31 woman.

My prayer for you as you read this book is that you will realize the importance of having a Life Plan, will glean ideas to apply in your own life, and will start living your life on purpose. In doing so I think you will find, as I did, that not having a Life Plan is like taking a trip without getting directions or having a map—you may eventually get where you want to go but at the expense of wasted time, talents, and energy. Why not pull off the fast track you've been traveling on and let God help you map out where to go from here?

Columnist Whit Hobbs says, "Success is waking up in the morning, whoever you are, wherever you are, however old or young, and bounding out of bed because there is something out there that you love to do, that you believe in, that you're good at—something that's bigger than you are, and you can hardly wait to get at it again today." Wouldn't you like to wake up every day and live out Hobbs's definition of success?

This book will help you do just that. I've formatted the book in such a way as to help you break down what might seem like an overwhelming project into manageable steps. It will require you to be in constant prayer, read God's Word in search of His will, write down Scriptures through which God speaks to you, develop your own fundamental life statements, set goals and action steps, develop a schedule, and examine your progress. You will need to be diligent and patient as you rely on God to direct you every step of the way. Remember Philippians 4:13, which says, "I can do everything through him who gives me strength."

Do not get overwhelmed but rather be excited about all God is going to reveal to you. In doing so, you will walk away with a Life Plan that I promise will dramatically change the way you see your life.

Section One

UNDERSTANDING THE FUNDAMENTAL QUESTIONS OF LIFE

Chapter One

WHAT WILL A LIFE PLAN DO FOR ME?

*D*o you ever feel as though you just don't have enough time? There is no changing the fact that there are sixty minutes in an hour, twenty-four hours in a day, and seven days in a week. However, in this age of dot-com everything, time rarely stands still. We have instant messages, instant dinners, instant coffee, and even instant grits. You can shop on-line, make friends on-line, and even take classes on-line with a virtual teacher. Kids are expected to grow up faster, the highway speed limit signs now allow us to drive faster, and everyone seems to have bought into the notion that faster is better. But is it?

Think about all we are doing. We wake up to *alarm* clocks. We *run* our errands. We get stuck in *rush*-hour traffic. We now meet friends in chat rooms and keep up with each other through voice-mail and E-mail. It's no wonder many of us start our days with a cereal appropriately named *Cheerios;* otherwise we might all go *Grape-Nuts!*

I'm not sure when all of this struck me. Maybe it was right after I drove off and left my groceries in the store parking lot. Or maybe it was the day I wore two completely different shoes and never noticed it until a friend was brave enough to tell me. Let's face it, we are all busy, but I just can't buy into the notion that we don't have time to do things that are really important. Take exercise, for example. All of us know we need to do it. We know the benefits, both physical and mental. Yet, the number one excuse people have for not exercising is lack of time. Another example is prayer. It's our direct connection to the God of the Universe, who longs to spend time with each of us, and yet we find ourselves too busy. I am just as guilty as anyone. What's the solution? I think it's found in writing out a plan and scheduling time to make it happen.

Have you ever noticed how focused you are and how much more you get accomplished right before you leave to go on a vacation? Why do you seem to be more energetic and focused? Why are you able to get a lot done in a short period of time? It's because you develop a plan with a goal in mind. Incidentally, did you know that most people give more thought and planning for vacations than planning their lives? Wouldn't it be great if you could live your life with that same passion and focus? Wouldn't it be awesome to have a plan that would enable you to get more accomplished during your day, meet your goals, realize your dreams, and live in peace knowing that you are living out the purpose for which you were created? For me, a Life Plan did this and much more.

A Life Plan Helps Add Value to My Life

Saint Augustine said, "People travel to wonder at the height of mountains, at the huge waves of the sea, at the long courses of rivers, at the circular motion of the stars—and they pass by themselves without wondering." A Life Plan will enable you to wonder at one of God's most amazing creations: you. You are a unique creation of God and He says you are wonderfully made. Your life is worth living on purpose! Developing your own Life Plan will help you ponder your purpose, discover your dreams, go for your goals, and realize firsthand that God has good things in store for you. It will help you organize priorities according to your purpose and put a value on the tasks you are spending your life accomplishing. The small investment of time that it takes you to develop and maintain this plan will pale in comparison to the amount of time you will gain. You will feel motivated to make every minute count as you get excited about where you are headed.

A Life Plan Helps Me See Life from an Eternal Perspective

Having a Life Plan has helped me to keep my focus where it needs to be. I can see the eternal significance of spending time with my Lord, loving my husband, caring for my children, being a keeper of my home, using my resources wisely, developing godly friendships, and reaching out to others. Then on those days when I start doubting whether or not I'm doing the right thing, I can look at my plan and get a quick reminder that there is an eternal perspective to be kept. When I cringe at how much baby-sitters cost, I remember how important my marriage is and consider the money spent a wise investment. Instead of looking at the diaper pail full of dirty diapers and seeing trash, I see a child whose physical needs have been met. When I'm cooking meals that I know will quickly be consumed and forgotten, I think about the value of family conversation and the lifelong memories made around our dinner table. You see, I am much more than a housekeeper, nanny, wife, friend, cook, chauffeur, decorator, businesswoman, family historian, events coordinator, coach, lover, exterminator, nurse, counselor, teacher, and personal playmate. I am a woman with a purpose, who has been created by God to fulfill a special calling. No one else is as uniquely qualified to fulfill my purpose as I am.

A Life Plan Helps Me Move Past My Mistakes

I wish you and I could sit down over lunch and share a heart-to-heart "girl talk." Since we may never get that chance, I want to share something from my heart with you. Every woman has messed up at some point in her life and done things she regrets. I used to think I was the only one with secrets from my past. This was Satan's bondage in my life and it made me think I could never be used of God. You see, I made a terrible mistake before I was married, and I got pregnant. I was terrified for anyone to find out because I knew all too well the sting of rejection. So I chose to go to an abortion clinic and ask for help. They told me that the procedure would be quick and that I would never have to think about this problem again. I bought their lie, and I have regretted it every day since. I long for that child and grieve over my tragic decision. Hardly a day goes by—even after all these years—that I don't think about it. However, God has set me free from the shame.

For me, answering the fundamental questions of life in my Life Plan helped me realize that I am not defined by my sin but rather by who God created me to be. I share this with you because I want you to know the hope that I have found. John 8:32 says, "You will know the truth and the truth will set you free." My friend, I pray that as you seek to develop your Life Plan, God's truth about who you are and how much He wants to use you for His glory will help set you free. I don't know what the circumstances of your life are, but I do know that nothing puts you beyond God's ability to forgive, heal, and restore.

A Life Plan Helps Me to See My Potential

A Life Plan helps bridge the gap between where I am today and where I want to see myself in the future. It gives me a place to start and helps reduce my regrets by measuring the progress I am making. I don't want to be complacent and give up hope of reaching my potential. I want to wake up every morning knowing that I am one step closer to hearing my Master say, "Well done, my good and faithful servant." A Life Plan gives me a tangible reference point to remind me of the wonderful potential I have as a child of the King. Ephesians 3:20 says, "Now to Him who is able to do immeasurably more than all we ask or imagine, according to His power that is at work within us." As a child of God, I have His power working in me, which increases my potential beyond my wildest dreams and highest hopes.

A Life Plan Serves as a Filter for My Decisions

A well-thought-out and prayed-through Life Plan serves as a filter that helps keep my focus where it needs to be when decisions must be made. I can ask myself, "According to my Life Plan, is this opportunity something that will help me fulfill my purpose? Does it make sense in light of how God has equipped me? Does it conflict with any of the principles I'm committed to living my life by? Is this the right season of my life to participate in this particular activity?" Just because something sounds like a worthy cause does not mean it is part of God's plan for me. There are and always will be thousands of good opportunities, but I am not searching for the *good*—I'm after God's *best*. I only have one shot at this thing called life, and it's worth it to give my best efforts.

A Life Plan Helps Point Me in the Right Direction

Whether you are married or single, with children or without, extroverted or introverted, rich or poor, young or old—you are a woman with a purpose and you were created by God for a divine reason. The key is to develop a plan clearly stating your foundation, purpose, mission, ministry, stage of life, and the principles by which you want to live. You will have your goals written down as well as the action steps and schedule that need to be implemented to insure your success. Then you will be headed down the right path and able to walk in confidence, knowing you have sought God and it is He who is directing you.

A Life Plan Will Help Me to Be Able to Give an Account on the Day of Judgment

First Corinthians 3:13 (LB) says, "There is going to come a time of testing at Christ's Judgment Day to see what kind of material each builder has used. Everyone's work will be put through the fire so that all can see whether or not it keeps its value, and what was really accomplished." Verses 14 and 15 (NIV) go on to say, "If what he has built survives, he will receive his reward. If it is burned up, he will suffer loss;

23

he himself will be saved, but only as one escaping through the flames." We will all be asked to give an account on the Day of Judgment of the life God entrusted us with. How sad it would be for God to ask what we did with our lives and for us to have no idea. Having a Life Plan will help you focus your efforts, make the most of the time you're given, and live according to God's purpose. Then you will hear your heavenly Father speak words that the heart of every one of His children longs to hear, "You did well, my child, with what I gave you and I am pleased."

A Life Plan Helps Me Rest in My Father's Arms

In the midst of all the craziness that sometimes surrounds us in life, there is a peaceful place to which we should often run. A place where we can find unconditional love. A place strong enough to hold any problem we are facing and gentle enough to wipe away our tears. This place is our Father's arms. Because our Life Plans will be bathed in prayer, based on God's Word, and filled with thoughts the Holy Spirit reveals to us, we will be able to rest in the fact that these plans are not our own. They will be what God chooses to reveal to you. It is because of His mercy and grace that we are able to do any of the things we write. Please do not ever think that these "works" are a way to earn salvation or your Father's love. Salvation is a free gift, and God's love is not based on what you do, but rather in the simple fact that you are His child. As His child, it should be your desire to please Him by being obedient to the Father's call to fulfill His divine purpose for you. Having a Life Plan will help you discover your purpose, live every area of your life according to this purpose, and rest in the fact that you are honoring God with your life.

These are just a few of the many ways you will benefit from developing a Life Plan. The best way to see how wonderful it could be for you is to simply get started and experience the benefits yourself. I remember the fear that I had when my husband first uttered the words *Life Plan*. It caused the same fear and panic I felt when I heard my OB doctor say the words *give birth*. All I could think of was pain and how much I try to avoid pain at all costs. Then I had a brilliant idea. Why hadn't women thought of this before? I asked him if he could please put me to sleep and wake me up when the baby was about five or so. Let's just skip the labor, the sleepless nights, the terrible twos, the first trip to the emergency room for stitches, the everything is "No!" phase, and start this motherhood thing around the time of kindergarten. Needless to say, I was awake for it all—and you know what? I wouldn't trade a second of it for anything. Just like giving birth, the labor to develop your Life Plan may not seem appealing but the end result will be nothing short of wonderful.

Just so you can have a picture of where we will be headed from here, I've diagrammed the process we will be going through to develop your Life Plan (excluding this chapter).

Section 1. Understanding the Fundamental Questions of Life

Chapter 2: The Fundamentals of a Life Plan

Chapter 3: My Foundation: "Who Am I?"

Chapter 4: My Purpose: "Why Do I Exist?"

Chapter 5: My Mission: "What Am I to Do?"

Chapter 6: My Ministry: "Where Am I to Serve?"

Chapter 7: My Stages of Life: "When Am I to Do These Things?"

Chapter 8: My Principles: "How Am I to Live Out My Day-to-Day Life?"

During chapters 3–8 we will be writing Fundamental Life Statements that will answer the life questions and lay the groundwork for writing the rest of our Life Plan in Section 2.

Section 2. Live Every Area of My Living on Purpose

Chapter 9: Finding P.U.R.P.O.S.E. in Each of My Principles.

Chapter 10: The Holy Pursuit: Finding My Purpose as a Child of God

WORKING ON YOUR JOURNAL

Throughout both sections of this book, we will be interacting with the companion workbook, *The Life Planning Journal for Women.* If you have this journal, you will benefit from the additional questions for a quick review of each chapter as well as plenty of space to journal and create your Life Plan. You will enjoy the ease of being able to record your prayers, thoughts, and plans on the beautifully designed pages. This easy-to-use journal will be an invaluable tool as you seek to apply what is discussed in *Living Life on Purpose.*

If you did not purchase *The Life Planning Journal for Women,* you will want to buy a three-ring binder and refer to the back of this book in Appendix A for directions on setting up you own journal. If you are making your own journal, transfer the questions given at the end of each chapter to that notebook and spend some time recording your answers.

Take time now to work on Section 1, Part 1, of your journal. Once you have completed your work in the journal, continue your reading by going on to chapter 2, "The Fundamentals of a Life Plan."

QUESTIONS TO CONSIDER IN YOUR JOURNAL

1. Have you ever stopped to wonder at the amazing way God has created you? Write down ten wonderful things about yourself. Don't let this be difficult. If you have a hard time, ask God to reveal the things He would have you write down.

2. Write out a prayer of thanksgiving to God for creating you as His special child.

3. God says you are wonderfully made. Journal your thoughts.

4. Choose three ways that a Life Plan could change your life from those listed in chapter 1 and journal how each could impact you personally.

5. What do you hope to accomplish through this study?

Chapter Two

THE FUNDA-MENTALS OF A LIFE PLAN

I was speaking at a retreat once where we played an interesting ice breaker game. As we walked into the registration room a mysterious sign was placed on our backs. We were told that we had just been assigned a new "famous" identity and that it was our job to figure out who we were based on the comments of others. Just for the sake of having a little fun, let's play. See if you can guess who you are by the following clues:

- People love you. (Mother Teresa?)
- You are very funny. (Erma Bombeck?)
- You have a handsome husband. (Whoever is married to Harrison Ford?)
- You are a little spacey. (Cindy Lauper?)

Well, even if you have not guessed who you are, I'm sure you've had a BALL playing the game (hint, hint). Yes, you are Lucille Ball.

For many of us, we are playing the very same game every day of our lives, never guessing the name on our back is our very own. In search of the *who, what, when, where, why,* and *how* answers in life, we seek to discover ourselves, but get lost in the process. I think life would be a lot easier if we all carried cards with us that listed the answers to all these questions about ourselves. Then we could cut through all the small talk and move right to the business of getting to know one another. OK, that is a bit extreme, but it does bring out an interesting point. If you were required to carry such a card, would you know how to fill it out? Can you answer these questions?

Who am I? (My Foundation)

Why do I exist? (My Purpose)

What am I to do? (My Mission)

Where am I to serve? (My Ministry)

When does God want me to do these things? (My Stages of Life)

How am I to live my day-to-day life? (My Principles)

When I first started the process of answering these questions about my life, the answers were less than beautiful. In fact, the description I came up with was so unattractive it is no wonder I had a hard time getting out of bed many mornings. My identity was like a tiny life raft tossed about in the sea. How I felt about who I was, why I existed, and what I was to do vacillated between positive and negative depending on how I perceived others were thinking of me at the time. If the waters were calm and serene, I drifted without direction, but at least above water. The danger came the moment a storm started brewing. I had no anchor, no compass, no hope. That was not what God had in mind when he said in Psalm 139:14 that we are "fearfully and wonderfully made." If God thinks I'm wonderful, who am I to question Him? He means for me to anchor my life to His truth, let His Word be the light that directs me, and find the hope that can only be found in having a personal relationship with Jesus.

As you consider your identity, imagine your life as a scale. The scale is tipped heavy to one side. The heavy side is all that you have been told about yourself by the world, your parents, and your peers. They have put a rock on their side every time they've said something negative about you. You are too fat. You are too loud. You aren't ambitious enough. You don't matter. In other words, you don't measure up to their expectations. The other side is what God says about you. The scale should be tipped heavily to this side. However, if you don't know what God says about you, there are no rocks to tip the scale in favor of His truth.

When you read God's Word, you find out that you do matter. Romans 8:31–35a says:

> What, then, shall we say in response to this? If God is for us, who can be against us? He who did not spare His own son, but gave him up for us all—how will he not also, along with him, graciously give us all things? Who will bring any charge against those whom God has chosen? It is God who justifies. Who is he that condemns? Christ Jesus, who died—more than that, who was raised to life—is at the right hand of God and is also interceding for us. Who shall separate us from the love of Christ?

Verse 39 answers this question with a resounding, "neither height nor depth, nor anything else in all creation, will be able to separate us from the love of God that is in Christ Jesus our Lord." We should fill God's side of the scale with so many rock-solid truths from His Word about who we are in Him that what others say will weigh like a handful of feathers.

God wants me to answer the fundamental questions of life based on His definition of me, not anyone else's. Understanding my identity in Christ was a major turning point in my life. God says that I am His holy and dearly loved child. God says that I am accepted in the beloved (Ephesians 1:6). God says that nothing can separate me from His love. Knowing that the God of the Universe loves and accepts me gave me a new perspective. Max Lucado says, "If God carried a wallet, your picture would be in it." I hope He does!

Because God thinks this highly of my life, so should I. Writing out these statements will help you stand for what you believe and keep you from falling into the subtle traps of discouragement, disillusionment, and defeat. It will also give you a written legacy to pass on to those who come behind you. And it will give you a reference to turn to when you feel knocked down and weary, reminding you that your life matters and your existence is important. Just like home base in the childhood game of tag, you run to home base, catch your breath, and find safety. There are days that I do just that. I pull out my Life Plan, re-read these life statements, curl up in my heavenly Father's arms and say a prayer of thanksgiving. I matter, and all of this is not for nothing, because God says so. I catch my breath and find safety before running back out into the game.

The next five chapters will help you think through these five basic questions of life. These fundamental statements are the starting point upon which you will build the rest of your Life Plan. Carefully consider each question and write from your heart. There are no right or wrong answers. Be assured the Life Plan Patrol will not seek you out and grade what you've written. Just start with simple but truthful statements. *Please note: This is not an exercise meant for you to use to beat yourself up over all that you are not.* You should write your statements without apology or regret. List your strengths with an attitude of thanksgiving that God has entrusted such wonderful gifts to you. Ask God to give you His perspective, and record what the Holy Spirit puts on your heart. I've included my statements at the end of each chapter for your reference.

WORKING ON YOUR JOURNAL

Take time now to work on Section 1, Part 2, of your journal. If you have *The Life Planning Journal for Women,* turn there now. (The questions listed below are already included in the journal itself.) If you are making your own journal, transfer the questions below to your journal and spend some time recording your answers.

Once you complete this section of your journal, continue your reading by going to chapter 3, where we will look at the most basic of the six Fundamental Life Questions: "My Foundation: 'Who am I?'"

QUESTIONS TO CONSIDER IN YOUR JOURNAL

1. What does it mean to anchor your life to the truth of who God says you are?

2. Draw out a scale as described in chapter 2. Is your scale tipped heavy to the side of what others say about you or heavy on the side of what God says about you?

3. Read Romans 8:31–35 and journal your thoughts about these verses.

4. Read verse 39 from this same chapter. Can anything separate you from the love of Christ? Journal your thoughts.

5. How could writing out your fundamental life statements help you?

Chapter Three

MY FOUNDATION: "WHO AM I?"

*W*hen I first accepted Jesus into my heart over twenty years ago I was happy to have religion in my life. I thought religion was just another aspect of being a well-rounded person. It took many years and many painful, lonely times to help me realize the need for a *relationship,* not a *religion.* An ongoing personal relationship with Jesus Christ must be the foundation upon which our lives are built. This relationship is the only thing that can give us the significance we spend our lives searching for. We have a void that must be filled, and I can now tell you that only God is big enough. Everything else I tried failed miserably and left me feeling hopeless and disillusioned.

I always thought that finding the right husband would fill my void and end my search for significance. I found a wonderful husband. I am convinced that I found the man God designed just for me and me for him. He's handsome, organized, successful, great with kids, and most important, very devoted to Christ. He loves me and I love him; however, that's not enough. When we were first married, I expected him to meet my every need and ease the ache I felt in my soul. He grew weary of trying and I grew impatient, angry, and confused waiting for a feeling that never came. Then I thought maybe children would be the answer. My kids are great. I could not feel more blessed by the daughters God has given me, but they could not fill my emptiness either.

Then came my quest for perfection. I thought that must be the secret. So I embarked on a journey to look perfect, act perfect, live in a perfect house, and pretend my life was nothing short of perfect. I remember one perfect day, I took my perfect children out to the mall. It was time for a new outfit because none of my old ones were making me feel perfect anymore. I found a few things to try on and proceeded to the nearest dressing room. I tried on a bright yellow blouse first. Deciding it was definitely not my color, I laid it aside and started trying on option number two. It seemed to have more potential, so I stepped out into the hallway to glance at the three-way mirror.

Suddenly, I heard a small familiar voice cry out, "Mommy, I have to go potty right now." I dashed back to the dressing room only to find my children locked inside. I bent down to see if I could crawl under the door but I couldn't fit. The space was large enough, however, for me to see my perfect daughter standing right over the yellow blouse that was now dripping wet. To make matters worse, my other daughter announced what happened to the entire store.

Needless to say, I bought the yellow blouse and left the store as quickly as possible. If this were to happen to me now, I would laugh and look forward to using the story in one of my seminars. Back then, even something as small as this sent me into a tailspin. My quest for perfection was like trying to build a house of cards in a windstorm. The harder I tried, the more frustrated I became. This frustration led to feelings of desperation. Finally, I hit bottom and had nowhere else to look but up.

People will always fail us at one time or another. Money can be lost in an instant. Successes can quickly be overshadowed by failures. But Jesus is and forever will be a solid foundation upon which to stand. The

Bible tells us in John 8:32 that "you will know the truth and the truth will set you free." Jesus is the truth, and He sets us free from hopelessness. He fills up the empty spaces in your life. He knows the story of your life has a happily-ever-after ending because He defeated the Enemy and claimed victory for all those who know Him! Does this mean that those who have an ongoing personal relationship with Jesus will never face hard times? No. Because the world has been tainted by sin, we will all face times of mourning, death, tears, fights, hurts, disappointments, and questioning. However, if my life is built on the solid foundation of God, I may be shaken at times, but I will never fall.

What is your life built on? Do you know the love of the father personally? Have you accepted Jesus Christ as Lord of your life? I would be doing you a disservice if I did not give you the opportunity to make this important decision right now. God does not expect you to be perfect in order to be a follower of Christ . . . you just have to accept the One who is. Come to Christ in prayer.

- Admit that you are a sinner, as each of us is sinful.
- Acknowledge Jesus as God's Son sent here to die on a cross to save you from your sin.
- Ask Jesus to be the Lord of your life and forgive you of your sin.
- Accept this free gift of salvation as something you have not worked for or earned. Now, all of heaven rejoices, as you have found your eternal home.

Whether you have been a Christian a few minutes or many years, it is vital for you to understand how to rely on Jesus as your solid foundation. The key is found in a daily personal walk with Christ. Through reading His Word, recording His Word in your memory, daily conversations through prayer, and finding accountability in your relationships with other believers, your solid foundation will form. You see, being a Christian should not just be a *part* of your life, it *is* your life. Letting Christ sit on the throne means that you release control and let Him govern how every part of your life is run. There is such peace—and believe it or not—*freedom* that comes through doing this. Jeremiah 29:11–13 says, "For I know the plans I have for you declares the Lord, plans to prosper you and not to harm you, plans to give you hope and a future. Then you will call upon me, and come and pray to me, and I will listen to you. You will seek me and find me when you seek me with all your heart." I can not think of any brighter plans than to let Christ give you a hope and a future. God also promises us in Hebrews 6:19 that "we have this hope as an anchor for the soul, firm and secure." He is a firm and secure foundation who will never fail us but will stand forever.

Now that we know the importance of our foundation being built on our relationship with Jesus, how do we come up with our own foundation statement? Your foundation statement answers the question "Who am I?" You cannot base this answer on your name, race, job, education, or social status. While all of those are valid descriptions, that is not what we are after here. This "who" question must describe the very essence of your being. Maybe a better way to prompt your answer would be to ask: "*Whose* am I?" Also include a sentence or two about your identity and self-worth. To lay the groundwork for each of the statements that will follow your foundation statement, you should simply state that you have a purpose, a mission, a ministry, seasons, and principles. End this section with a brief summary of how you view your life. I've included my foundation statement below for your reference.

My Foundation: I am a child of God. This is who I am. My relationship with Jesus Christ is not merely the religion compartment of my life but rather the foundation that everything else in my life is built on and around. My identity is solid. God calls me a holy and dearly loved child who is adopted as one of His very own. Because of this, I should never question my self-worth. God sent His only son to die on a cross to save me from my sin so that I could spend eternity with Him. There is purpose to my existence, value in the mission I am to accomplish, a ministry that needs my service, and seasons of life to be enjoyed. I am committed to living by my seven basic principles, so that I can be all that God intended for me to be. My life is a gift from God. Living a life that honors God and draws others to know and love Him is my gift back.

WORKING ON YOUR JOURNAL

Take time to work on Section 1, Part 3, of your journal. If you have *The Life Planning Journal for Women,* turn there now. (The questions listed below are already included in the journal itself.) If you are making your own journal, transfer the questions below to your journal and spend some time recording your answers.

Once you complete your foundation statement, continue your reading by going on to chapter 4, where we'll look at the next Fundamental Life Question: "My Purpose: 'Why Do I Exist?'"

QUESTIONS TO CONSIDER IN YOUR JOURNAL

1. Do you have a personal, growing relationship with Jesus?

2. Is there a void in your life that you have tried to fill with people or things? What have you attempted. Explain.

3. Has there been anything that has been able to fill you completely? What have have you attempted? Explain.

4. Are you relying on God to meet all your needs?

5. Read John 8:32. What does the truth of Jesus need to set you free from?

6. Read Jeremiah 29:11 and record it here.

7. What promises does God make to you in this verse?

8. According to Hebrews 6:19, the hope found in Jesus serves as an _____ for the soul that is _____ and secure.

9. What foundation is your life built on?

Chapter Four

MY PURPOSE: "WHY DO I EXIST?"

After answering the very important foundation question, "Who am I?" the next logical question is "Why do I exist?" The answer to this question is your purpose in life. Everything else that we will do to develop our life plan is based on this purpose. Every other fundamental life statement depends on a solid purpose. You see, we must first understand *why* we exist in order to answer the *what, where, when,* and *how* questions.

Henry Ford, founder of The Ford Motor Company, said, "The whole secret to a successful life is to find out what it is one's destiny to do, and then do it." Knowing that I have a purpose and being able to define what that is has given me a passion for living that I never had before. My soul is drawn, my spirit is lifted, and I can't wait to jump out of bed each morning in order to press on in the great race of life. Maybe you are not so eager most mornings. Maybe you are like I was for so many years, and you find it very difficult to face each new day. Well, let me share a story to encourage your heart.

A group of refugees was about to flee a war zone by hiking over some of the most rugged terrain in their country. As they were about to leave, they were approached by a frail old man and a sickly mother who carried an infant. The leaders of the group agreed to take them along with the understanding that the men would take turns carrying the baby, but that the mother and the old man would have to make it on their own.

Several days into the journey, the old man fell to the ground, saying that he was too exhausted to continue and pleading to be left behind to die. Facing the harsh reality of the situation, the leaders of the group reluctantly decided to do just that and started on their way.

Suddenly, the young mother placed her baby in the old man's arms, told him that it was his turn to carry the child, and walked away with the group. It was several minutes before she allowed herself to look back, but when she did, she saw the old man stumbling along the trail with the child in his arms.[1]

The old man now had a purpose, and it gave him a reason to live. Suddenly, his focus changed from dying to living. The baby in his arms needed him to get up and keep walking. Even more so, he needed the baby to give him a reason to do so. He found the courage to continue, the strength to persevere, and a will to survive.

Maybe you are sitting on the sidelines ready to let life pass you by or maybe you are like the old man, ready to call it quits. Well, it is not time to give up. It's time to stand up, take hold of your purpose, and keep on walking. I believe every person was created by God for a specific purpose. Romans 8:28 says, "And we know that in all things God works for the good of those who love him, who have been called according to his purpose." You have a purpose. It's the reason you exist. There are three key components to your purpose as found in Romans 12:1–8:

- Declare your master.
- Determine your mind-set.
- Describe and develop your makeup.

Using these three components as your guide will help you write a solid purpose statement.

Declare Your Master

Romans 12:1: "Therefore, I urge you, brothers, in view of God's mercy, to offer your bodies as living sacrifices, holy and pleasing to God—this is your spiritual act of worship."

Your body in this verse is more than just your physical being. It includes your spiritual being as well. We are to voluntarily give our whole selves to God in a holy and pleasing way. We declare God as our Master worthy of devoting our lives to. We are to surrender our sinful desires in pursuit of holiness and allow God to use us as instruments with which He can carry out His perfect plans. Proverbs 3:5 says, "Trust in the Lord with all your heart and lean not on your own understanding; in all your ways acknowledge him, and he will make your paths straight." Because God is my master, I know He will lead me on the right paths and I am assured of my eternal destination.

Declaring who your master is, is the first step toward defining your purpose. In my kitchen, just above my sink, I have a small brass plaque that serves as a reminder that my household will serve the Lord. The scriptural basis for this statement comes from Joshua 24:15, "Choose for yourselves this day whom you will serve. . . . But as for me and my household, we will serve the Lord." Joshua commanded the Israelite people to declare their master. To help the people remember that they chose the Lord, He recorded their response and set a stone in place to bear witness to their commitment. We should do the same. Declare your master, write in into your purpose statement, and then place a reminder somewhere in your home to hold you true to your commitment.

Determine Your Mind-Set

Romans 12:2: "Do not conform any longer to the pattern of this world, but be transformed by the renewing of your mind. Then you will be able to test and approve what God's will is—His good, pleasing and perfect will."

I am not a seamstress; however, in moments of temporary insanity I have tried to "grasp the spindle." Let's just say my works did not bring very much praise. I have great respect for my friends who sew, and to my amazement I have discovered what helps them create such fine garments and beautiful bed coverings. They use a pattern. What a novel idea. I've never been much on reading directions, so when it came to following a pattern I was a bit challenged. OK, I admit I never even took it out of the package. I just looked at the picture on the front of the package and gave it my best shot. My results were not at all like those of my detail-oriented, pattern-following friend, Sharon. Her work is amazing.

Well, when you follow a pattern, your workmanship will produce the product of the pattern. According to Romans 12:2, we have a choice of patterns in life. If we choose to follow the world's pattern, we will become like the world. However, if we choose to follow God's pattern, our minds will be transformed to become like the mind of Christ. What should our mind-set be? Our thought pattern should be determined by God's Word. Philippians 4:8 says, "Finally, brothers, whatever is true, whatever is noble, whatever is right, whatever is pure, whatever is lovely, whatever is admirable—if anything is excellent or praiseworthy—think about such things." Romans 12:2 goes on to instruct us that after we renew our minds using God's pattern we will be able to know what God's good, pleasing, and perfect will is. That is why our mind-set is a crucial component of our purpose statement. We must know what the will of our Master is if we are to do what He has put us here to do. Don't look to the world for your purpose. Look into God's Word. Let your mind be transformed day by day. This is part of our purpose—to get alone in silence with our Master and seek His will every day. Don't seek to fill in this part of your purpose with details of the tasks to be completed. God will reveal those over time. This part of your purpose statement should be your commitment to seek God with all of your mind and to make the most of every opportunity He blesses you with.

Describe and Develop Your Makeup

Romans 12:3–6: "For by the grace given me I say to every one of you: Do not think of yourself more highly than you ought, but rather think of yourself with sober judgment, in accordance with the measure of faith God has given you. Just as each of us has one body with many members, and these members do not all have the same function, so in Christ we who are many form one body, and each member belongs to all the others. We have different gifts, according to the grace given us."

The Holy Spirit gives us spiritual gifts in seed form. They must be used to serve others in order for us to grow and flourish. There is a spiritual depth that cannot be reached until we tap into the rich resources given to us. A good picture of this concept can be learned by the story of a man named Yates who owned a sheep ranch in Texas. It was during the Great Depression, and he was struggling even to put food on the table. One day, an oil company knocked on his door wanting to know if they could drill on his property. They promised that if they struck oil, he and his family would receive a large portion of the profits. Yates agreed. After drilling over eleven hundred feet, they struck one of the richest oil reserves in Texas, and Yates and his family became instant millionaires. Now, let me ask you an interesting question. Was Yates rich before the oil company came knocking? Yes, and so are we. If only we would tap into the rich potential of our God-given gifts, we too could be transformed overnight.[2]

Now that you have declared your master and determined your mindset, you are now ready to complete the third component of your purpose statement: describing and developing your makeup. Romans 12:3–6 teaches us that because of God's grace, He has given each of us different gifts. These gifts are listed in verses 6 through 8 as *prophecy* (preaching), *serving, teaching, encouraging, giving, leadership,* and *mercy.* There are three other major passages of Scripture where gifts are mentioned: Ephesians 4:11; 1 Peter 4:9–11; 1 Corinthians 12:1–11, 27–31. Please note as well that there are other passages that mention gifts not included in these lists.

The gifts found in those passages include *evangelism, missions, apostle, wisdom, discernment, knowledge, hospitality, shepherding, music, intercession, healing, miracles, praying with the spirit* (tongues and interpretation), *administration,* and *faith*. If you have never studied spiritual gifts, please refer to Appendix B in the back of this book for an explanation of each that may help you better understand your gifts. If you would like to do a more in-depth study, other resources are listed for your reference.

These gifts of the Spirit should not be confused with the fruits of the Spirit as found in Galatians 5:22–23. Gifts reveal *ministry,* whereas fruits show *maturity.* God gives us these gifts to equip us to serve in ministry opportunities and help fulfill a specific function within the Christian body. Every believer has at least one gift, and it is your responsibility to develop your gifts. We should always remember that our gifts are not given to us so that we can brag about all that we do. They are given so that we can serve others. Our attitude should always be one of thanksgiving that God has chosen, by His grace, to entrust us with such special responsibilities.

My Purpose: My purpose for existing is to be in constant fellowship with Jesus so that he can shape and mold me to be like Himself. In my day-to-day life, I desire to seek God as I live intentionally and make the most of every opportunity that He gives me. I believe I was created to be used as a vessel through which God can encourage and equip others to become all that He intended for them to be. I have been blessed with special abilities to write and speak. I feel passionate about using my gifts of evangelism, teaching, and wisdom to be a woman of godly influence in the lives of my husband, my children, and others whom I touch.

WORKING ON YOUR JOURNAL

Take time to work on Section 1, Part 4, of your journal. If you have *The Life Planning Journal for Women,* turn there now. (The questions listed below are already included in the journal itself.) If you are making your own journal, transfer the questions below to your journal and spend some time recording your answers.

Part of this journal entry is to work on your own purpose statement. Write down all of the things I've just mentioned that will assist you. Whether you are using the printed journal or your own, remember to *declare your Master, determine your mind-set,* and *describe and develop your makeup.* spend time in prayer and ask God to help you write out a clear and concise purpose statement.

Once you complete your purpose statement, continue your reading by going on to chapter 5, where we'll look at the next Fundamental Life Question: "My Mission: 'What am I to Do?'"

QUESTIONS TO CONSIDER IN YOUR JOURNAL

Your Purpose

1. Read Romans 12:1–8.

2. Record Romans 12:1.

Your Master

3. How do you consider yourself to be a living sacrifice?

4. Are you pursuing holiness? Give examples from your life.

5. How are you seeking to be pleasing to the Lord with your life?

6. Read Proverbs 3:5. Are you trusting the Lord, as this verse instructs?

7. Read Luke 16:13 and record it here.

8. Are you trying to serve more than one master?

9. Joshua commanded that the people choose the Lord (Joshua 24:15). He recorded their response and set a stone in place to bear witness to their commitment. We should do the same. Declare your Master by writing it below.

Your Mind-set

10. Record Romans 12:2.

11. What are some ways you are conforming to the pattern of this world?

12. How can you be transformed?

13. What will be the benefit of renewing your mind?

14. You must know what the will of your master is if you are to do what He has put you here to do. Don't look to the world for your purpose. Look into God's word. Let your mind be transformed day by day. This is part of our purpose, to get alone in silence with our Master and seek His will everyday. Don't seek to write this part of your purpose with details of tasks to be completed. God will reveal these over time. This part of your purpose statement should be your commitment to seek God with all your mind and make the most of every opportunity He blesses you with. Determine your mind-set by stating in writing what you will allow to be the pattern for your mind.

Your Makeup

15. According to Romans 12:3–6, are you needed by the other members of Christ's body?

16. If you were to describe yourself as body part, what would you be and why? (An eye? An ear? A leg?)

17. Have you tapped into the rich potential of your God-given gifts?

18. According to the Scripture passages that list the spiritual gifts, what are your spiritual gifts? (Remember to read Appendix B in this book for a listing of all the gifts and a description for each.)

19. How are you using these gifts?

20. Our gifts are not given to us so that we can serve others. Our attitude should be always be one of thanksgiving that God has chosen, by his grace, to entrust us with such special responsibilities. How are you serving others with your gifts?

21. Write out your purpose statement taking note of the guidlines given above concerning this statement.

Notes

1. Joseph P. Klock, essay in *Personal Selling Power*, November-December 1993. © Copyright 1993 by *Selling Power*. Reprinted by permission of the publisher.
2. Information taken from a story told by Bill Bright in *How You Can Be Filled with the Holy Spirit* (Arrowhead Springs, Calif.: New Life, 1991), 28–29.

Chapter Five

MY MISSION: "WHAT AM I TO DO?"

I remember the day I caught my first glimpse of what my mission in life would be. I was sitting in my den with tears streaming down my cheeks staining the pages of the Bible study book I held in my hand. The question I was trying to answer for that week's lesson dealt with whether or not I would do whatever God asked of me. At first my answer was, of course, whatever God wants me to do, I'll do.

As I attempted to go on to the next question, I felt God speaking to my heart, "Will you share your testimony?" In a panic I closed the book and started praying out loud. I told God I would do anything except share the painful experiences from my past. A picture popped into my head of all the people who would reject me if they knew the secrets of my past. No way, not in a million years, would I ever be able to share my testimony. Besides how could God use my junk for His glory?

I felt God again speak to my heart, "What the devil meant for evil, I will use for good. Trust me, Lysa, trust me." I knew I was at a major crossroads in my spiritual journey. God was pointing in one direction, and I was running in the opposite direction. I had to decide whether or not I was going to obey God. By the end of our time together I reluctantly told God that at my next speaking engagement I would share part of my testimony. A few weeks later I stood before a group of women and did just that. Tear-stained faces all over the room confirmed that this was a message women needed to hear. God used the story of a broken vessel to pour out His love, comfort, and compassion. Several women were saved and over half recommitted their lives to Christ. I witnessed a miracle of God that day and I have never been the same.

As I drove home that evening, I told God that I would go to the ends of the earth and share everything about my life with whomever would listen. I have kept my promise, and so has God. What the devil meant for evil, God truly has used for His glory. This is the mission God has for me in my role as a servant of Christ. I am to be a transparent person who allows God to take the pain of my past and use it as a bridge that others may walk from darkness into His wonderful healing light.

I want women to know that God desires to use them as well. You see, we all have a story. Things have happened in our lives where only God could comfort us. We are responsible to pass on God's comfort to others. Remember—God doesn't comfort us to make us comfortable. He comforts us to make us comfort-*able:* able to be used as vessels through which God can pour out his mercy, love, and comfort to others. Let me ask you the question that changed my life: *Are you willing to do whatever God asks of you?*

I love the story about a little boy and his grandfather walking along the beach after a storm. Hundreds of starfish had washed up on the shore and the little boy was busy picking them up and throwing them back into the water. The grandfather asked the little boy why he was doing this because he could not possibly save them all. The little boy looked at the starfish in his hand and replied, "No, but I can make a difference in the life of this one." You'll never know what kind of difference you can make until you surrender your desires for your life to the perfect mission God has for you.

In order to get a clear vision of your mission, you must understand three important biblical truths. You are a new *creation* of God, who has been *chosen* by God, to fulfill a *calling* from God. God has uniquely equipped you to answer the calling of your mission. You have been given **e**xperiences, **q**ualifications, **u**nique spiritual gifts, **i**nterests, and a certain **p**ersonality type. Notice that when you take the first letter of each of these words, they spell E.Q.U.I.P.

Experiences

Have you ever asked God, "God, why did you let this happen to me?" I have asked this question so many times. I have asked it in times of sorrow as well as times where I have made a complete fool of myself. My life has been such a comedy of errors at times. I now know that God gave me all these things so that I could empathize with those in pain and share funny stories letting people know how very real I am. God has given you experiences to use for His glory as well. The wonderful thing for Christians is that God promises us that He will work all things together for the good of those who love Him. James 1:2–4 says, "Consider it pure joy, my brothers, whenever you face trials of many kinds, because you know that the testing of your faith develops perseverance. Perseverance must finish its work so that you may be mature and complete, not lacking anything."

Imagine sitting down at a table with two cups of flour, three eggs, a tablespoon of vanilla, one cup of sugar, one teaspoon of baking powder, and a few other ingredients. You taste the sugar and it is good, but when you taste the baking powder it is bitter. You continue to taste the ingredients, some tasty and some downright gross. This is like life. Some of the events in your life are sweet like the sugar, others dry like the flour, and others still that you don't like at all. However, using Jesus' perfect recipe, all of the events in your life will be mixed together and put through some intense heat—and then you will rise. Just as a cake would not be the same if you left out some of the ingredients, so Jesus wants to use all of your experiences to make you complete and able to be used for His glory.

Qualifications

Your qualifications are your skills and abilities, those things that you do well either through training and education or natural ability. Exodus 31:3 gives us the example of God telling Moses that He has given a person skills, abilities, and knowledge in all kinds of crafts.

Now before you say that you have no skills or abilities, let me assure you that the average person possesses around six hundred skills and abilities. The key is to match your abilities with a place of ministry. For example, some of Jesus' disciples were fishermen. The ability to catch fish was something they were skilled at. Jesus called these men to use their fishing abilities to become fishers of men. They could use what they were already good at in a place of ministry. Not that they would actually haul in loads of people with nets, but rather that they knew how to cast nets that would attract. So instead of fishing nets, they cast out the Word of God into the hearts of people.

An example from my life is the ability to write poems. This is something I use to express through rhyming words pictures of life that touch people's hearts. My friend Glynnis has the ability to edit. Whereas she used to use this skill in the workplace, she now uses it in ministry by editing the newsletter of the Proverbs 31 Ministry, *The Proverbs 31 Woman*. Another friend of mine, Lynn, has the ability to decorate for events in such a way that makes people feel welcome and special. There are many different abilities from accounting to public relations to teaching aerobics. Take time to start a list of your abilities that might be used in some way to glorify God.

Unique Spiritual Gifts

These are gifts, *your* gifts, which we listed as your makeup from the third component of your purpose statement. Remember—these gifts are given to us in seed form. We must cultivate and use these gifts to see them develop. One of my gifts is evangelism. I love to share the gospel with people, and God gives me the most wonderful opportunities to do so.

About a year ago we had a second phone line installed in our home that was only one digit off from the long distance information line in a certain region of South Carolina. At first I was so frustrated with the influx of callers wanting phone numbers to Bud's Seafood and Bessie's Best Bathing Suit Shop. Just as I was about to call the phone company and demand they fix the problem immediately, God reminded me of my commitment to make the most of every opportunity He gives me.

So the "God line" was born. I started proudly answering the phone, "God-line information. We don't have all the answers but we know the one who does. How may I help you?" Most of the time I get a bewildered "Huh?" on the other line, but every now and then God uses this wrong number to set divine appointments with Him. (By the way, my other home number is only one digit off from the local pizza parlor. God has such a sense of humor!) Let me encourage you to look for ways to cultivate your gifts. I can promise you will see them grow and flourish.

Interests

You have two types of interests: intense interests and fun interests. Intense interests are topics or issues that you feel passionate about. If you were given an opportunity to address the world for one hour on prime-time television, what would you talk about? If I had this chance, I would share my testimony about my abortion. Not to condemn those who have had one but rather to offer them the hope and healing that I have found through Jesus. I would also encourage anyone who is considering an abortion to have an ultrasound and see for herself the tiny heart that beats within the little unborn child. I would tell them that although this child may seem like a mistake to them, it is not a mistake to God. God has great plans for this baby. He will bring people to help pregnant girls who feel alone and afraid. This is my intense interest.

Your interests also consist of things you consider fun. If you had an entire day to do anything, what would you do? Well, for me, I'd go skiing with friends and family. Don't ask me how as a native Floridian, I acquired such a passion for hitting the slopes. It just happened. I'm hooked. This is one of my fun interests and what I'd do if given a free day.

Personality

This is the way you express yourself and relate to other people. Some of us are introverts, whereas others of us are extroverts. Some of us are task oriented; others are people oriented. You have been given a wonderful personality perfectly suited for what God intends for you to do. I am an extroverted, people-oriented person. I love to have fun—so let's play a quick game. Put this book down for just a minute and get your lipstick tube. Do you have it in hand? (I'll bet if you're like me, you ran to get your lipstick and got sidetracked somewhere between your purse and the junk drawer in your kitchen. It has probably taken you several hours to make your way back to this book. If you're one of those task-oriented people, you've probably skipped this game and are sticking to the task of reading the rest of this chapter.) OK, pull out your tube and examine its shape. According to a very "official" lipstick personality chart given to me at a church retreat, you might discover that your lipstick really can tell a lot about you.

Group one: Flat-top lipstick people: To the point, high morals, conservative, very dependable

Group two: Rounded, smooth-tip lipstick people: Easy-going, peacemaker, steady, generous

Group three: Sharp-angled-tip lipstick people: Opinionated, high-spirited, outgoing, likes attention

Group four: Sharp-angled but curved-tip lipstick people: Creative, enthusiastic, energetic, talkative, loves attention, falls in love easily, needs a schedule but dislikes one

Group five: Sharp angles on both sides lipstick people: Curious, mysterious, faithful, looks for the easy way, loves life

Group six: Keeps slant close to original slant and tip shape lipstick people: Abides by the rules, great follower, does not like too much attention, somewhat reserved, likes a schedule

Remember, no matter what shape your lipstick or what kind of personality you have, the key is to discover your personality's attributes and make the most of those while seeking to improve on your personality's weaknesses.

This special EQUIPment is for you to use to help you fulfill God's calling in each role you play. For each stage of your life, you will be required to play different roles. As you choose the roles you will play, you need to limit your commitment to no more than four major roles. In my life, I have chosen to be a servant of Christ, a wife, a mother, and a friend.

While your roles may differ from mine, you should focus your energy on making the most of your major roles. You should apply the 80/20 rule. You should dedicate 80 percent of your time to your four major roles and 20 percent of your time to other less significant roles. After you decide what your four major roles are, pull out your calendar and see if your schedule matches your calling.

When I did this I found a source of great frustration in my life. I was wasting significant time on insignificant things. For example, my calendar was filled with meetings for things that were not part of my calling. I finally realized that life would not stop if I pulled out of some of those activities. You see, too many of us are too busy to find our mission in life. We are consumed with participating in everything, and as a result we are not effectively making a difference in anything.

Others are at the opposite extreme of this and are not doing anything. Either out of feelings of inadequacy or laziness, they simply sit on the sidelines of life and watch as others pass by. Both of these are tragic situations. Life should not be something that just "happens" to you; it should be something that you live to the very fullest, determined to do all that God created you to do.

In the parable of the talents found in Matthew 25:14–30, Jesus told of a master who entrusted three servants with a certain number of talents. One servant, who was given five talents, decided to invest his talents and earned the master's praise and respect. Because the servant had been faithful with a few talents, he was given more. The servant who was

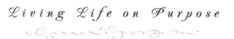
given two talents also earned his master's praise and respect for investing wisely and getting a return on his investment. However, the third servant was called wicked and lazy for burying the one talent he had been given and not doing anything productive with it. His talent was taken from him, and he was cast out into darkness. Which servant can you identify with?

God has entrusted us with much. He has given us life, and He wants to see that we are investing our lives wisely. I don't know about you, but I want to make my Master proud. I long to hear, "Well done, My good and faithful servant." To those who give good accounts and live their lives wisely, God will affirm their efforts with encouragement, and He will entrust more to them. Do you want to live an abundant and fulfilling life? Invest your talents wisely. Use what God has given you to fulfill your purpose and answer the call of your mission.

My Mission: In my role as a servant of Christ, I have been called to be a transparent person who is willing to share my life experiences, both good and bad, and to live a victorious Christian life that draws others to Christ. As a wife, I have been called to be my husband's helpmate and complete him so that he can be the man God wants him to be. As a mother, I have been called to be a Christlike example to my daughters while instilling in them strong character, biblical values, and the desire to follow Christ. As a friend, I am called to love and give of myself to make life a sweeter experience for those I touch.

WORKING ON YOUR JOURNAL

Take time to work on Section 1, Part 5, of your journal. If you have *The Life Planning Journal for Women,* turn there now. (The questions listed below are already included in the journal itself.) If you are making your own journal, transfer the questions below to your journal and spend some time recording your answers.

Part of this journal entry is to work on your own mission statement.

When writing your mission statement, include a sentence for each of the major roles you are currently in. Try to limit those major roles to no more than four. Write down what you feel God is calling you to do in each of those areas.

Once you complete your mission statement, continue your reading by going on to chapter 6, where we'll look at the next Fundamental Life Question: "My Ministry: 'Where Am I to Serve?'"

QUESTIONS TO CONSIDER IN YOUR JOURNAL

1. Are you willing to do whatever God asks of you?

2. How does the statement, "What the devil meant for evil, God can use for good," apply in your life?

3. Using the acrostic "EQUIP," list the five ways God will equip you for your mission:

Experiences

4. Read James 1: 2–4 and record it.

5. What are some of the trials you've faced?

6. How have these trials made you more mature and complete?

7. How have these experiences helped equip you for a mission

Qualifications

8. What are some of your skills and abilities?

9. How do your qualifications help equip you for your mission?

Unique Spiritual Gifts

10. Look back at the makeup section of your purpose statement.

11. What spiritual gifts did you list there?

12. Do you feel you are seeing your spiritual gifts grow and flourish? If yes, how? If no, how can you develop them past their seed form?

Interests

13. How do your spiritual gifts help equip you for your mission?

14. What are some of your intense interests?

15. What are some of your fun interests?

16. How do your interests help equip you for your mission?

Personality

17. Are you more of an introverted person or extroverted person?

18. Are you more of a task-oriented person or a people-oriented person?

19. Do you think God would call you to do something that might challenge your natural personality traits? Why?

20. How does your personality help equip you for your mission?

21. List the four major roles you feel called to at this time of your life. For each role write a sentence or two about how you might best utilize what you've been equipped with in each role.

22. To those who give good accounts and live their lives wisely, God will affirm their efforts with encouragement and will entrust more to them. Do you want to live an abundant and fulfilling life? Invest your talents wisely. Use what God has given you to fulfill your purpose and answer the call of your mission. Write out your mission statement, including a sentence for each of the major roles that you are currently in. Write down what you feel God is calling you do in each of these areas.

Chapter Six

MY MINISTRY: "WHERE AM I TO SERVE?"

*M*atthew 5:16 says, "Let your light shine before men, that they may see your good deeds and praise your Father in heaven." One of my favorite childhood Christian songs sang about not hiding our light but letting it shine, shine, shine. Though I've never tried to hide my light, I have been through many phases of life where my light was not very effective. The first, my "drifting phase," was characterized by the word *complacency*. My light was like a swinging lantern. It gave off light, but because it was not focused in any one direction, it was not very efficient light. This was the time where I drifted in and out of service projects. I served strictly because there was a need. But because these were projects I had not been called by God to take part in, I grew weary and tired. I had a hard time keeping my commitment to the project once the newness of it wore off, and many times I quit, letting down others and myself.

The second phase I moved into was my "determined phase," which was characterized by the word *complaining*. My light was like a spotlight, which was more focused but in the wrong direction. I had the spotlight pointed at me. I was determined to win the lost and encourage my fellow saints by letting everyone see how perfect my life was and how hard I was working. This light was not effective, either, because instead of drawing people to Christ, I turned them off by my unrealistic act. I was always complaining that no one appreciated my efforts. What I failed to realize is that our good deeds should bring glory to our Father in heaven, not ourselves.

Finally, I have been "delivered," the third phase. My life and ministry are now characterized by the word *committed*. What made the difference was getting down on my knees before the Lord and asking Him to show me where He wanted me to serve. I then waited and watched for my answer. I did not proceed until I felt God specifically calling me to join Him where He was at work. My light is now as focused as a laser, able to cut through the darkness of this world and pierce even hearts of steel. The amazing thing about a laser is that it does not necessarily take more energy to produce such powerful results. It just takes an intensified focus. I am serving both where I am called and where I am needed. I have focused in on three ministries: my home, teaching children in my church, and the Proverbs 31 Ministry.

The key to effective ministry is to focus your efforts where God is calling you and stay plugged into God! If I took a lamp and set it on a table, would it magically start shining? I could put in the most powerful light bulb, but it wouldn't shine until it was plugged into the energy source. The first place you must get plugged in is with God. You see, in order for you to pour your life into the lives of others, God must first fill you!

Mother Teresa said, "We need to find God, and He cannot be found in noise and restlessness. God is the friend of silence. See how nature—the trees, the flowers, the grass—grows in silence; see the stars, the moon and sun, how they move in silence. The more we receive in silent prayer, the more we can give in our active life. We need silence to be able to touch souls. The essential thing is not what we say, but what God says to us and through us. All our words will be useless unless they come from within—words which do not give the light of Christ increase the darkness." What wisdom there is in what she is saying. You can't give more than you've been given.

Let me encourage you to pull back from all of life's busyness and get alone in silence with God. Psalm 46:10 says, "Be still, and know that I am God." God wants us to come to him, calm our bodies and our minds, and know that He is in control. He has made you to serve and knows where you should be serving. Ask Him specifically where you should go and what you are to do. When I did this, God was faithful to answer me. Because I now know that I am serving where He made me to serve, I love what I'm doing and have no problem staying committed to the cause. Paul had this same assurance in his ministry. In his letter to the Philippians, he wrote, "One thing I do: Forgetting what is behind and straining toward what is ahead, I press on toward the goal to win the prize for which God has called me heavenward in Christ Jesus" (Philippians 3:13b–14).

The second place we must get plugged into is a ministry. Matthew 20:28 says, "Just as the Son of Man did not come to be served, but to serve, and to give his life as a ransom for many." We know we have been created, chosen, and called to a mission. We have been equipped for our mission by God. Now it's time for us to put action to our mission and get plugged into a ministry. Just like Jesus, we are called to our ministry to serve and not to be served.

There are three characteristics of a servant that we should have when serving in our ministry. The first is *submission*. We must be willing to submit to God's calling and know that we are accountable to Him for the job we do. The second is *selflessness*. We should give of ourselves without expecting recognition for our service. The third is *sacrifice*. We must be willing to give of our time, energy, and resources. We will have to sacrifice the desires of the flesh in order to fulfill the service of the Father.

Are there rewards for service? Is it worth the necessary sacrifices? Yes, my friend, there are many rewards and it is worth the effort. The rewards here on earth are what I call "fulfillment blessings." The satisfaction that you are doing what God created you to do will give you a sense of fulfillment like nothing else. Giving to others will fill your empty places. Do you feel depressed? Reach out to those who are less fortunate than you, and you will feel your depression melt away. Do you feel lonely? Reach out to someone who is truly alone, and you will find company. Do you feel worthless? Reach out to someone whom society has labeled as an outcast, and you will know you are needed.

Remember how I told you that God called me to share my testimony? Well, as I shared earlier, part of my testimony talks about my heartbreaking experience with an abortion. The grief and overwhelming shame of this part of my life was so hard to come to terms with. I had asked God to forgive me, gone through countless counseling sessions, and read books that dealt with recovery and healing, but still the pain was unbearable. For me, it took the sacrifice of my "perfect" image and the submission of my plans to God to finally find peace. Because I allowed God to get into the secret places of my heart, He has healed me, washed me white as snow, and now uses me to help others.

Yes, it is hard to share my story with others. But I know that there are children alive today because God has used my story to tell the truth about the tragedy of abortion. This has been what has helped me heal. I now know that my child's life was not for nothing. Isaiah 61:3 says, "To bestow on them a crown of beauty instead of ashes, the oil of gladness instead of mourning, and a garment of praise instead of a spirit of despair." God has redeemed the ashes of my life and bestowed on me a crown of beauty.

Do I deserve His merciful response to me? Absolutely not. So why would my Father give such unmerited favor to His children? It is called *love*. While we benefit greatly from this love, we cannot possibly understand its depth. So even out of my sin, God was able to work good. Because I have been obedient to share my story as God called me to, many have heard about Christ's love, forgiveness, and hope. Many have accepted Jesus and will be in heaven because of God's working through this tragic situation. Allowing God to use me in this way has filled me with peace and assured me that God truly can use everything for his eternal purposes. Seeing God work miracles through my painful experiences has given me a peace that nothing else could.

There are also heavenly rewards. The rewards you will receive in heaven will be more precious than anything your eye has seen or your ear has heard. Paul said it best as he was nearing the end of his service.

Second Timothy 4:7–8 says, "I have fought the good fight, I have finished the race, I have kept the faith. Now there is in store for me the crown of righteousness, which the Lord, the righteous judge, will award to me on that day—and not only to me, but also to all who have longed for his appearing."

Just think, it will be like winning the Miss America Pageant times one thousand. You'll walk up to the God of the universe and He will put on your head a crown of righteousness. Then as you bow before all His majesty, you will lay your crown at the foot of your Savior. You will thank Him for allowing whatever it took in your life to bring you to this moment where you see Him face-to-face. You will realize that while the works you accomplished may have been good and necessary, they pale in comparison to the importance of the relationship the two of you have.

Your relationship with God is your ultimate reward here on earth and in your eternal home in heaven. To borrow from my friend Sheila Mangum in her book, *Dancing with Daddy,* "Then you will take the hand that created you. You will hold the palm that has your name written in it. You will be in the arms that you have run to many times. You will dance on the feet that guide you to all truth. You will look into the eyes that watched you every second of your life. You will touch the face of love and dance down the streets of gold with your Bridegroom."[1] That's your reward. Not because you deserve it. Not because any of the works you have done have earned it. Just because Jesus loves you.

My Ministry: I am fulfilling my purpose and answering the call of my mission by serving in my home, my church, and through the Proverbs 31 Ministry. I am making my home a safe haven where my family can find a loving wife and mother who meets their physical and emotional needs. At church, I serve where I am gifted (in evangelism and teaching) and where I am needed (in the children's ministry). Through the Proverbs 31 Ministry, I am touching women's hearts and helping them to build godly homes through my writing, speaking at conferences and on the radio, and by serving in the leadership of the ministry.

WORKING ON YOUR JOURNAL

Take time to work on Section 1, Part 6, of your journal. If you have *The Life Planning Journal for Women,* turn there now. (The questions listed below are already included in the journal itself.) If you are making your own journal, transfer the questions below to your journal and spend some time recording your answers.

Part of this journal entry is to work on your own ministry statement. Whether you are working on your own or through the printed journal, take care to see that your statement clearly states where you are fulfilling your purpose and answering the call of your mission. You should include the place you are serving, both where you are needed and where you are gifted. Remember to include a brief description of how you are helping others through your ministry opportunities

Once you complete your ministry statement, continue your reading by going on to chapter 6, where we'll look at the next Fundamental Life Question: "My Ministry: 'Where Am I to Serve?'"

QUESTIONS TO CONSIDER IN YOUR JOURNAL

1. Which of the three phases (drifting, determined, or delivered), can you most identify with? Why?

2. What is the key to effective ministry? What does that mean for your life?

3. Read Psalm 46:10 and record it here.

4. When are you still before the Lord?

5. Read Matthew 20:28. Just like Jesus, you are called to your ministry to _____ and not to be _____.

6. List the three characteristics of a servant.

7. To whom must you submit?

8. Define selflessness.

9. What will you have to sacrifice?

10. Are there rewards for serving?

11. Write out your own ministry statement noting the directions given above for completing this assignment.

Note

1. Sheila Mangum, *Dancing with Daddy* (Phoenix: ACW: 2000), 134.

Chapter Seven

MY STAGES OF LIFE: "WHEN AM I TO DO THESE THINGS?"

*I*saiah 61:3 says that God will give us beauty for ashes, gladness for mourning, and peace for despair. He does this so we can be called oaks of righteousness, a planting that glorifies Him. Just like a tree, we will go through different stages while experiencing the seasons of life. In order to continue our growth and persevere through each of the spiritual seasons of life, we must be firmly planted. Psalm 1:3 says, "He is like a tree planted by streams of water, which yields its fruit in season and whose leaf does not wither. Whatever he does prospers."

Every oak starts out as a small acorn. As the acorn develops into a small seedling, roots will form. It is vital to the tree's survival for its roots to get firmly established and have a regular water supply. Then and only then can the small tree grow and persevere through all of the seasons. The same is true in our lives. God wants us to be oaks of righteousness. Not well-intentioned acorns. Not seedlings that might some-day grow. No, we are to be firmly rooted oaks that draw nourishment from God's living water and grow to glorify Him by the fruit we pro-duce.

When I was a little girl I remember seeing the stump of a tree that had been cut down. I was told that if I counted the rings on the stump's surface, that I would know how old the tree was. Wider rings reflect years of abundant rainfall and growth. Narrower rings show that there might have been a drought or some other shortage of water, thus less growth for the tree. Based on the scars within the rings, you can also see if a tree has been attacked by insects or affected by a fire. Probably the most interesting fact about tree rings is that the tree must go through a dormant season, usually in the fall and winter, for these rings to form. This still fascinates me. Our growth through each stage of life should be just this obvious. We need to be able to identify what stage of life we are in and seek to make the most of the opportunities available to us in each stage.

There will also be limitations according to the stage you are in. We need to balance our priorities so that we meet the responsibilities each stage requires while continuing to press on toward fulfilling our purpose, answering the call of our mission, and serving in ministry opportunities. Too many people use their stage-of-life limitations as excuses to put serving God on hold. The problem with this is that every stage of life has its limitations and excuses. For example, I used to dread teaching children's church. Being the mother of young children, that was the last thing I felt like doing on Sunday. I wanted to sit in the sanctuary and have someone minister to me. However, God showed me that it was a privilege to minister to young children and that He could teach me valuable life lessons through them. Matthew 18:5 says, "Whoever welcomes a little child like this in my name welcomes me."

I am so thankful I did not miss out on welcoming Jesus all those Sundays. You see, if we wait to serve God until we are in an easier stage of life, then we might not ever serve Him. Let me encourage you to move past excuses and into prayerful consideration of what kind of service would fit within the priorities of your life.

It is also important to note that within each stage of life you will experience various spiritual seasons. We love the spring season when leaves are green, the air is warm, and the buds are on the trees. Then summer comes, and the heat is intense and we are uncomfortable. If we are not careful to take in plenty of water, our leaves will wilt and start to fall. When the fall comes, we lose our leaves, the air turns cool, and we feel bare and cold. Then the winter dawns, and we feel its presence in the bitter winds and gray skies. We tend to think of this dormant season as a curse, when in reality the winter is a blessing. God uses the dormant times to make us be still, turn our eyes to Him, and allow Him to make distinct marks on our lives. Just as for the tree, the dormant times are when our life rings form. Finally, without warning, tiny buds start to form and the sun shines again. Spring has returned, and we sway and rejoice in the warm spring air.

Although each season is not equally rewarding, each is necessary for growth. Which season can you identify with? Are you flourishing and producing lots of fruit? Are you under one of life's pressures and feel the heat of the refiner's fire? Are you being stripped of something where your branches feel bare? Are you in the middle of a crisis where life seems cold and empty?

Let me assure you, no matter what stage and season of life you are in right now, God wants to use you. God wants to teach you. He wants to fill you. He wants to pour Himself into you so that you can then be used to fill other people with His love. Don't be discouraged, but rather encouraged about all God is doing with your life right where you are.

When I had my third child, my life went from full to overflowing. I knew adding this new joy in my life would require letting other things go. I was in a fall season, where it was time to let go and give up some things. I felt God was calling me to step out of my role as president of the Proverbs 31 Ministry. I trusted God and let go. The winter soon came with all its bitter cold. I felt confused in my new role as vice president because I was no longer involved with every decision and in every project. I felt left out and lost. God just kept telling me to hang on and trust Him. I did just that, and when spring came it brought with it the opportunity to write this book. If I had not been willing to persevere through the fall and winter, I would have missed out on a most glorious spring. During my dormant season, God made some distinct marks on my life pattern and now I am so thankful to be one ring closer toward becoming a full-grown oak of righteousness.

The stage of life you are in is significant and the spiritual season necessary. Make the most of every blessing you have. Realize that the stumbling blocks you seem to trip over at times may actually be stepping stones leading you closer to God's glory. Vince Lombardi said, "I firmly believe that any man's finest hour—his greatest fulfillment to all he holds dear—is that moment when he has worked his heart out in a good cause and lies exhausted on the field of battle—victorious." No matter what field of battle you are on, work your heart out for God in this stage and season. Your finest hour is coming.

My Stage of Life: I am a wife and mother of three young daughters. My schedule is hectic at times because of the physical needs of my family, but tremendously exciting. As I am learning to serve and meet the needs of my husband, God is teaching me the value of submission, the rewards of a servant attitude, and how wonderful love is when He is at the center of a relationship. Through my experiences as a parent, God has allowed me to more clearly understand His love for me. He loves me even more than I love my children. Therefore, He must discipline and teach me just as I discipline and teach my daughters. At this stage of my life, I must make a conscious effort to make the most of every minute so that I will be able to balance the demands of ministry while giving my family all that they deserve from me. In order to manage my life effectively, I must schedule my time according to my priorities.

WORKING ON YOUR JOURNAL

Take time to work on Section 1, Part 7, of your journal. If you have *The Life Planning Journal for Women,* turn there now. (The questions listed below are already included in the journal itself.) If you are making your own journal, transfer the questions below to your journal and spend some time recording your answers.

Part of this journal entry is to work on your own stage of life statement. Whether you are working on your own or through the printed journal, consider these questions as you prepare this statement.

- What roles are you currently playing and what are your responsibilities?
- What is God teaching you through each of the roles that you play?
- What are your time limitations?
- How will you keep your priorities straight?

Once you complete your stage of life statement, continue your reading by going on to chapter 8 of this book, where we'll look at the last of the Fundamental Life Questions: "My Principles: 'How Am I to Live Out My Day-to-Day Life?'" In that chapter we will defne the principles that will help you structure the second half of your Life Plan.

QUESTIONS TO CONSIDER IN YOUR JOURNAL

1. Read Isaiah 61:3 and record it.
2. Why does God give us beauty for ashes, gladness for mourning, and a praise for despair?
3. According to Psalm 1:3, where are we to draw our nourishment from?
4. How do the rings of a tree relate to a person's life?
5. What would the rings of your life look like? Take time to draw them and journal a brief description about each.
6. We need to seek to make the _____ of the opportunities available to us _____.
7. Which season can you identify with at this time in your life? Why?
8. No matter what stage and season of life you are in right now, God _____ you!
9. Why does God want to fill you?

10. The stage of life you are in is significant and the spiritual season necessary. Make the most of every blessing you have. Realize the stumbling blocks you seem to trip over at times may actually be stepping stones leading you closer to God's glory. With all this in mind, write out your stage of life statement, considering the bulleted questions given above.

Chapter Eight

MY PRINCIPLES: "HOW AM I TO LIVE OUT MY DAY-TO-DAY LIFE?"

We will design the rest of our Life Plan based on the model of the Proverbs 31 woman described in Scripture. Proverbs 31 features a woman who finds the delicate balance between her activities and her family. Since I find myself struggling with this at times, I decided to glean from her wisdom and experience. I think her secret is twofold. First, her strength comes from the Lord. She is not dependent on other people, circumstances, or worldly securities. She is clothed with the strength and dignity that only comes from a heart that is filled with God alone. She does not get caught up in comparing herself and her works to others. She does the best with what she has and lives her life seeking only to reverence the Lord. I know that the Lord will never give me more than I can handle, so the first step to finding balance is to seek the Lord and His direction for my family and my activities.

The second step that must be taken is to clearly define your principles and make sure you set your priorities accordingly. Using Proverbs 31 as a guide, the Proverbs 31 Ministry has established solid principles for any woman desiring to be a Proverbs 31 woman. I would encourage you to use these principles for this section of your Life Plan. If some of these principles do not apply at this point in your life, concentrate on the ones that do.

The Seven Principles of the Proverbs 31 woman:

1. The Proverbs 31 woman reveres Jesus Christ as Lord of her life and pursues an ongoing, personal relationship with Him.

2. The Proverbs 31 woman loves, honors and respects her husband as head of the home.

3. The Proverbs 31 woman nurtures her children and believes that motherhood is a high calling with the responsibility of shaping and molding the children who will one day define who we are as a community and nation.

4. The Proverbs 31 woman is a disciplined and industrious keeper of the home who creates a warm and loving environment for her family and friends.

5. The Proverbs 31 woman contributes to the financial well-being of her household by being a faithful steward of the time and money God has entrusted to her.

6. The Proverbs 31 woman speaks with wisdom and faithful instruction as she mentors and supports other women and develops godly friendships.

7. The Proverbs 31 woman shares the love of Christ by extending her hands to help with the needs in her community.

Before we go any further, I think it would be helpful to take an in-depth look at the Scriptures that describe our friend of virtue. Proverbs 31:10–31 is structured as an alphabetic acrostic using the twenty-two letters of the Hebrew alphabet that applauds this honorable woman. Let's look at her characteristics using the letters of the English alphabet.

Admired: *"Her children arise and call her blessed; her husband also, and he praises her"* (v. 28).

I used to wish I had an instruction manual on marriage and motherhood. One that described in specific detail how to make my husband so happy with me as a wife that he would sing my praises. One that instructed me how to raise each of my children so that they would rise up and call me blessed. Then I realized that God had done this through the Bible. My instructions are clear. I must read and heed the godly advice given. I must also be patient as God takes me and my family through the assembly phase one step at a time. Then in due time I will receive my blessings.

Business-minded: *"She makes linen garments and sells them, and supplies the merchants with sashes"* (v. 24).

She is following that old saying: "Waste not, want not." She has made more than her household needs, so she is selling her extras to benefit her family financially. The same principle can be applied in our homes today. We can either sell our extras at garage sales and consignment stores or supply those who would benefit from them by donating them to charities. Some women have also found it financially rewarding to open up small businesses out of their homes to contribute to the family budget.

Careful with her finances: *"She considers a field and buys it"* (v. 16a).

Speaking of budgets, there is no better way to contribute to the financial well-being of a family than to carefully manage the finances. As keepers of the home, one of the most important things we do is to keep watch on how we spend the money God has entrusted to us. Especially for larger purchases, to carefully consider means to weigh out whether this is a want or a need, whether or not this is the appropriate time to make such a purchase, and whether or not we are being wise stewards of God's money. Like the Proverbs 31 woman, we should carefully consider our purchases, commit to sticking to a budget, and let God be the Lord of our life and Lord of our checkbook.

Dressed for success: *"She is clothed in fine linen and purple"* (v. 22b).

The Proverbs 31 woman made her own fashion statements, literally. This sewing woman could whip together threads that would have rivaled most fine dress shops. I found this quite intimidating as the only thing that my sewing needles do well is pick out splinters. Even though I don't make my own clothes, I do make a conscious effort to dress appropriately. I think it's interesting that she wore purple, which is a sign of royalty. We are daughters of the King, and our outer and inner beauty should reflect our royal heritage.

Early-Riser: *"She gets up while it is still dark"* (v. 15a).

The Proverbs 31 woman is not the only biblical person who got up while it was still dark. Jesus did so to spend time with the Father. There is such value to rising early, giving God the first fruits of our day, and preparing ourselves spiritually for all that our day holds.

Financially savvy: *"She sees that her trading is profitable, and her lamp does not go out at night"* (v. 18).

I was what you might call challenged in the area of finances when Art and I first got married. His first big mistake was giving me a credit card to be used for emergencies. When we got the bill at the end of the month, Art questioned my many emergencies. The problem was in how we defined the word *emergency*. His definition was a flat tire. Mine was a one-day sale at my favorite department store. In order for the Proverbs 31 woman to see that her trading is profitable, she must keep a watch on her finances. Whether you are trading stocks, buying groceries, or furnishing your home, remember to budget wisely and leave your credit cards at home during those one-day sale emergencies.

Generous: *"She opens her arms to the poor and extends her hands to the needy"* (v. 20).

I love the mental picture this verse gives me. As she opens her arms, she is exposing her heart. Because her heart is filled with gentleness, kindness, compassion, and love, she can't help but reach out and touch the ones in need around her. Luke 6:45a says, "The good man out of the good treasure of his heart brings forth what is good"(NASB). The Proverbs 31 woman keeps a careful watch on what fills her heart because she knows it is the wellspring of her life. The overflow of our hearts can only pour out Christ's love if we are filled with Him first.

Helpmate for her husband: *"Her husband is respected at the city gate, where he takes his seat among the elders of the land"* (v. 23).

Have you ever heard someone say that behind every great man is a really great woman? Well our Proverbial friend may have been the first to coin the phrase. Have you ever thought about all the great things your husband might be capable of if he got the right kind of encouragement? We can choose whether we want to be our husband's chief critic or chief cheerleader. Men need respect and admiration from the one they love. These two essentials can fuel a man past the pitfalls of life and right into a respected position at the city gate.

Investor: *"Out of her earnings she plants a vineyard"* (v. 16b).

You definitely could not call me "Stockbroker Sally." However, I have learned to be a wise investor. My investments are nothing that would interest Wall Street, but I am getting great returns. I have decided to invest my life for eternity's sake. I am especially committed to three blue chip stocks named Hope Amelia, Ashley Suzanne, and Brooke Caroline. The Proverbs 31 woman wisely invested her earnings in a vineyard because that would enable her to continue to increase her gain. That is why I am investing myself into the lives of my three daughters. I can continue to increase my "heavenly gain" by leaving a legacy of Christlike love for my daughters to pass on to the generations who come behind me.

Jewel: *"She is worth far more than rubies"* (v. 10b).

My little girls love to play dress up. They love to be transformed into princesses and pretend our home is a fairy-tale castle. I love for them to play this childhood game because when they play like princesses, they act like princesses. Did you know that you are a princess of the Most High King? He calls you His child. Do you embrace your royal heritage and let your position in Christ define your self-worth? The Proverbs 31 woman is worth far more than rubies, not because of the things she does but because of *whose* she is.

Keeper of the home: *"She watches over the affairs of her household and does not eat the bread of idleness"* (v. 27).

Being a keeper of the home means much more than cleaning house. It means watching over the physical and spiritual needs of those who need your home to be their haven. Our homes should be safe places where things like criticism, condemnation, and cynicism are strictly forbidden. As keepers of the home, we must be available to kiss scraped knees, listen to broken hearts, and watch for opportunities to cheer our families on in this great race of life.

Loyal: *"She brings [her husband] good, not harm, all the days of her life"* (v. 12).

Genesis 2:18 tells us that God made the wife to be a suitable helper for her husband. We are to come alongside our husbands and help them to become all that God intends for them to be. We have the choice to either be a complainer or completer. If you choose to complete your husband, you must be willing to pray and ask the Lord to change the things about your husband that you feel need to change. Then leave those things with the Lord and be willing to let Him change your heart if He chooses not to change your husband. Your responsibility is not to fix your husband, but to be the best partner you can be and let God do the rest.

Mentor: *"She speaks with wisdom, and faithful instruction is on her tongue"* (v. 26).

No matter how old you are, there are younger women that would benefit from your life experiences. If you are a young mother, there are teenage girls that could benefit from your advice on dating and finding the right mate. If your children are older, new mothers are desperate for encouragement and helpful hints from those of us that have been in their shoes. Mothers with teens need empty nesters to give tried-and-true adolescent advice. There is never a time in life when others would not benefit from your coming alongside them and offering help. The most important thing to remember when seeking to mentor others is that you cannot take anyone else any further then you have already been. In other words, in order to give wisdom and faithful instruction, you must first acquire these yourself.

Noble character: *"Many women do noble things, but you surpass them all"* (v. 29).

A noble character is worthy to be followed. I know I must be careful with the footprints I leave because little feet are scampering right behind, gingerly placing their feet into my prints. Wherever I am traveling, so are they. To have a noble character is to reflect the qualities of a king. My King has walked the same paths of life that I am now on and has left a map for me to follow. I must remember to clutch His words in my hands and heart, seek to follow His leading, and make sure of where I'm headed.

Optimistic: *"She is clothed with strength and dignity; she can laugh at the days to come"* (v. 25).

There is no better feeling than to wake up excited about the gift of a new day. The Lord tells us that we should rejoice and be glad for the day He's made for us. However, many people have a dark cloud of depression, hurts, disappointments, and failure that cast gray skies over their days. It is hard to laugh at the days to come when you can barely drag yourself out of bed in the mornings. The Proverbs 31 woman is clothed with the strength and dignity that comes from keeping an eternal perspective on life. She knows God is in control and that He has good plans for her. She chooses to have an optimistic attitude, knowing that while she can't control her circumstances, she can choose how she reacts to them. Since her life is anchored to her trust in God, no matter what storms she may face, she will still be standing, able to smile at the days to come.

Prepared: *"She provides food for her family and portions for her servant girls"* (v. 15b).

The Proverbs 31 woman does a lot to provide for her family. She cooks, she cleans, she sews, she plants vineyards, and best of all, she is not afraid to ask for help. One of the best things I've ever done for my sanity and that of my "Mr. Clean" husband was to find a mommy's helper to lend me a hand. While our budget would not allow for much, we did manage to afford a reasonable hourly rate for homeschool students who wanted a little extra spending money. Over the years, I have realized the value of being willing to ask for help. No one benefits from me trying to be a super-hero, do-it-all-myself, lone-ranger woman.

Qualified: *"Give her the reward she has earned, and let her works bring her praise at the city gate"* (v. 31).

This verse is the reason we press on through all the ups and downs of womanhood. Here she finally reaps all the good she has sown throughout her life. Sometimes when we are knee deep in dirty diapers, homework projects, one of those not-so-fun marital discussions, and trying to make gourmet meals out of boxed macaroni and cheese, we lose perspective on why we are doing all of this. I know I've caught myself getting weary and wondering, *Am I making any kind of difference in the lives of those around me?* Galatians 6:9 says, "Let us not lose heart in doing good, for in due time we will reap if we do not grow weary" (NASB). Those who sow good seeds can rest assured there is a blessed harvest ahead.

Ready: *"When it snows, she has no fear for her household; for all of them are clothed in scarlet. She makes coverings for her bed"* (v. 21–22a).

I'll never forget the snowstorm that dumped over a foot of snow and ice on us and knocked out our electricity for nearly a week. With temperatures dropping into the teens, I was very grateful for our Y2K generator. My husband and I decided to make the investment for a generator because we felt God put it on our hearts to be prepared in case of a possible computer crisis at the turn of the century. When the New Year 2000 came and went without a hitch, we wondered if we had heard God wrong and made an unwise investment. However, as I tucked my children into their warm beds in the middle of the icy storm, I thanked God for helping us know how to be prepared. We may not know how to be prepared for all that lies ahead of us; that's why it's important to stay in touch with the One who does.

Strong: *"Her arms are strong for her tasks"* (v. 17b).

I used to think the only reason a person needed to sweat was if he were lying out in the sun. I never liked exercising and frankly avoided it at all costs. However, when I met my exercise-loving husband, I decided to impress him, so exercise became a part of my daily routine. I'll never forget the first day of our honeymoon when he asked me whether I wanted to run or bike that day. I told him neither, and I revealed my true feelings toward moving my muscles. Well, I've come full circle now, and I actually enjoy working out. I have found that the benefits help me physically and mentally to better handle my daily tasks. I am not sure that they had Nike running shoes and aerobic classes back in the days of the Proverbs 31 woman, but I do know that she, too, enjoyed the benefits of keeping her arms strong for her tasks.

Trustworthy: *"Her husband has full confidence in her and lacks nothing of value"* (v. 11).

Confidence in a person can only happen through commitment. The important thing to remember about commitment is that it is a decision, not a feeling. Too many people are giving up on their marriages today because they've lost that "loving feeling." This is tragic. Feelings will come and go in a relationship like the tide of the ocean. Making the decision to commit for better or for worse will lead to good feelings, not the other way around. Let me encourage you to resolve to never make decisions regarding your relationship based on feelings but rather rest on the solid commitment you made to each other and the sovereign covenant you made with God. Then you and your husband both will have full confidence in one another and your marriage will lack nothing of value.

Unique: *"In her hand she holds the distaff and grasps the spindle with her fingers"* (v. 19).

The Proverbs 31 woman had unique hobbies she enjoyed where she could express her creativity. While holding the distaff and grasping the spindle is not my idea of fun, I do like making scrapbooks and writing poetry. I think it is good for a woman to find a hobby that she can enjoy during her down time. Which brings me to an important point—we all need down time. Time to get alone and do something just for ourselves. This isn't selfish; it's the smart way to avoid burnout. Whether you are a career woman with a million to do's or a mom with small children scampering about, let me encourage you to find a way to take mini-retreats and do something fun just for you. You'll discover that you are able to give more once you've taken a little time to rejuvenate yourself.

Vigorous: *"She sets about her work vigorously"* (v. 17a).

In order to set about your work vigorously you must be energetic and effective. Have you heard the saying, "Don't work harder, work smarter"? Well, the Proverbs 31 woman was a smart worker. She chose to plan ahead, get up early to start her days off the right way, and to take pleasure in all she did. We all have choices. We can choose to be negative or set about our work with the right attitude and be energetic and effectively vigorous.

Works with eager hands: *"She selects wool and flax and works with eager hands"* (v. 13).

Have you ever caught yourself working with less than eager hands? Hands that grumble, complain, and wonder if anyone appreciates all their hard work? I know I have. However, I know God sees and appreciates all we do for those we love. He says that when we do for the least of them, we do it for Him. So, whether you are selecting wool and flax, scraping mystery food from the floor under your kitchen table, grabbing the dashboard of the car your teen is learning to drive, or once again trying to find those matching socks the dryer must have eaten, do it with eager hands unto the Lord.

Excellent cook: *"She is like the merchant ships, bringing her food from afar"* (v. 14).

If Proverbs 31 were written today, this verse would probably read: "She is like a mini-van, bringing her food from the grocery store and a few fast-food joints." I am all for home-cooking, but there are some days where it is just not possible. On those crazy days, I think it's perfectly fine to zip through a drive-through. The most important thing about bringing your family food is the quality time spent together around the dinner table. Meaningful memories can be made while eating home-made-mashed or French-fried-potatoes.

Yields her life to the Lord: *"Charm is deceptive, and beauty is fleeting; but a woman who fears the Lord is to be praised"* (v. 30).

God isn't telling us through this Scripture that outward beauty is bad. He is saying that it can be deceiving and it doesn't last. Have you ever seen fresh ginger? Next time you are at the grocery store, take a peek. On the outside it appears anything but beautiful. However, once you strip off the outside layers, what lies underneath is wonderful. That's what God wants from us. He wants our inside to be so filled with Him that we can't help but be beautiful because our beauty comes from within.

Zenith: *"A wife of noble character who can find?"* (v. 10a).

This ultimate woman is missing in action. She's the finest and the greatest. Many are searching for her. Could you be the missing woman? I think so. Sharon Jaynes reminds us of the relief we can find in knowing that that the one word we cannot find in Proverbs 31 is the word *perfect*.[1] You don't have to be perfect to qualify. You just have to know the One who is!

WORKING ON YOUR JOURNAL

Take time to work on Section 1, Part 8, of your journal. If you have *The Life Planning Journal for Women,* turn there now. (The questions listed below are already included in the journal itself.) If you are making your own journal, transfer the questions below to your journal and spend some time recording your answers.

Once you complete your Stage of Life Statement, continue your reading by going on to chapter 9. Now that we've outlined our principles and examined the Proverbs 31 woman's many admirable qualities, we'll discuss in chapter 9 how to find P.U.R.P.O.S.E. in each of the seven principles of the Proverbs 31 woman.

QUESTIONS TO CONSIDER IN YOUR JOURNAL

1. Proverbs 31 features a woman who has found the delicate balance between her _____ and her _____.

2. Do you struggle finding this balance sometimes?

3. The Proverbs 31 woman was able to find this balance because: her strength comes from _____ and she has clearly defined her _____ and sets her _____ accordingly.

4. List the Seven Principles of the Proverbs 31 woman

5. Pick three of the Proverbs 31 woman's characteristics that you would like to improve upon in your own life. List them and describe how you would like to improve in each area.

Note

1. Sharon Jaynes, Epilogue, *The Best of the Proverbs 31 Ministry: Encouragement and Inspiration for Women* (Charlotte, N.C.: The Proverbs 31 Ministry, 1999), 295.

Section Two

LIVING EVERY AREA OF MY LIFE ON PURPOSE

Chapter Nine

*F*INDING
P.U.R.P.O.S.E
IN EACH OF
MY PRINCIPLES

*N*ow that we have a picture of the Proverbs 31 woman and the seven principles she personified, we can proceed with the completion of your Life Plan. With each of the seven principles, we will be using the word *purpose* as an acrostic to help establish the steps we'll need to take so that we can live every aspect of our life on purpose. The word P.U.R.P.O.S.E. stands for:

Pray,

Understand God's Word,

Record key Scriptures,

Plan goals,

Outline action steps,

Set a realistic schedule, and

Examine your progress.

Pray

Before we seek to do any planning in each aspect of the seven principles, we must first pray. We must dedicate each area to God and ask for His guidance and direction. Then we will have the blessed assurance that it is God who is establishing these plans and not us. Acts 5:38b–39a says, "For if their purpose or activity is of human origin, it will fail. But if it is from God, you will not be able to stop these men." Nothing can hinder you from living every area of your life on purpose if God has established your plans. Four reasons prayer is key to a Life Plan:

1. *We must ask first and then we will receive.* Matthew 7:7–8 says, "Ask and it will be given to you; seek and you will find; knock and the door will be opened to you. For everyone who asks receives; he who seeks finds; and to him who knocks, the door will be opened." If we do not receive, we must go back to God in humble submission to get our motives right. James 4:3 reminds us that sometimes we don't receive when we ask because we ask with wrong motives. A few verses later, in James 4:10, the Scripture says, "Humble yourselves before the Lord, and he will lift you up." The best way to humble yourself before the Lord is to get down on your knees before Him. God desires to give good gifts to us but we must ask with the right motives in mind.

2. *We need to be in constant communication with the one who wants us to prosper and have hope for our future.* Jeremiah 29:11–12 tells us that God has good plans for us, ones that are full of hope. If we want to know God's best plans, we have to talk with Him as we walk with Him every day.

   What a difference it has made in my life to learn how to be in constant communication with my heavenly Father. Those days that I'm weary and discouraged, God is so faithful to give me little reminders of His love and demonstrate that He cares for me in the most amazing ways. Other days, when life is wonderful, everything is a little sweeter because I share it all with God. I feel the warmth of my Father's touch both when He's wiping my tears as well as when He's high-fiving the good times. He's truly my friend who sticks closer than a brother. If you've never known this kind of relationship with God, take time to develop your prayer life and watch amazing things happen.

3. *In order to succeed, we must commit to God all that we do and all we hope to do.* Proverbs 16:3 says, "Commit to the Lord whatever you do, and your plans will succeed." We need God. We need His provision and His protection as we apply each of the seven principles to our lives. By committing everything to God, we are placing our future in hands that will insure our success. We are saying that no matter what happens, we trust God and want to live out His definition of success, not the world's definition.

4. *God wants to become very real to us.* At the lowest point in my life I found help through attending a post-abortion Bible study at the local Crisis Pregnancy Center. Because my shame was so overwhelming, I could not drive myself. I couldn't bear the thought of someone seeing my car parked in the parking lot and wondering why I was there.

Most of the time my husband was available to take me; however, on one of the days when I had to drive myself, God arranged a divine appointment. I don't remember exactly what happened as I drove to the Bible study that day, but I do remember slamming into the car in front of me. As the man from the other car approached my crumpled vehicle, I fixed my eyes on his wild blond hair. Amazingly, he never concerned himself with the damage done to his car. He just came up to me, asked if I was all right, and told me not to worry about his car. He instructed me to still go to the place I was headed to before the accident and then, as quickly as the accident happened, he was gone.

I knew at that point that everything was going to be all right. Somewhere in the midst of all the car engines I was almost sure I heard the brush of an angel's wings. Why would I share that story with you? Because more than anything God wants us to realize that He desires to be intimately involved with every aspect of our lives. The way we invite Him to do this is through prayer.

Throughout that Bible study I had been praying for God to become very real to me and show me that He really did love me. After that car accident I have never doubted Him or His love again. I parked my crumpled car right in front of the Crisis Pregnancy Center and walked into my Bible study ready to meet with my Redeemer that day.

As you apply each of the Seven Principles demonstrated by the Proverbs 31 woman, you'll want to write out specific prayers. First you will want to acknowledge and adore God, then have a time of confession, then move into prayers of thanksgiving, and finally move to supplication, where you present prayer requests. This is the most important step in developing a plan for each area of life. It will be a wonderful time of fellowship with God and focusing on the needs of the precious people with whom God has blessed your life.

Understand God's Word

God's Word is filled with wisdom and wonderful promises. If we seek to understand God's Word and let it permeate every area of our lives, the transformation will truly be remarkable. Romans 12:2 says, "Do not conform any longer to the pattern of this world, but be transformed by the renewing of your mind. Then you will be able to test and approve what God's will is—his good, pleasing and perfect will." In looking at your Life Plan, one of the most essential aspects to consider is God's will—His good, pleasing, and perfect will. So how do you find out what that will is?

You will be transformed by having your mind renewed with God's Word. It is essential to get into the Bible and discover what God's Word says. The closer we align our thinking to God's Word, the better off we are in making life decisions. If we want to know God's will, we must make understanding His Word a top priority in our life. For each principle area of our Life Plan, we will seek to understand what God's Word says and how He intends for us to live out each aspect of life.

Record Key Scriptures

Think back in your life and recall times where you felt very close to the Lord and the Scripture passages that became very meaningful to you during these times. I call these spiritual markers because they are times from your past where God has clearly spoken to you through His Word. Have you ever read a passage of Scripture, felt particularly touched, and knew that it was a nugget of truth that you needed to hear and apply? That is the voice of God. That is our Heavenly Father reaching down from His eternal throne to care specifically for one of His precious children. That's your Daddy talking. Don't you think what He has to say is vitally important? I do. I think it's important enough to record on paper so I can read it over and over until it is permanently written on my heart.

Martin Luther said, "I know not where He leads me, but well I know my guide." As God guides us, we should keep track of these markers. He's leading us, teaching us, and preparing us for great things ahead. He has our purpose in mind! This is one of the areas of our Life Plan that we should be continually adding to. Each time you experience a spiritual marker in your life, pull out this section of your Life Plan and write it down. You will be amazed at how much your faith will grow from the evidence of God working in specific ways in your life. Here's a sample of how I recorded a key Scripture and journaled the spiritual marker I gleaned from His truth:

Galatians 1:10 asks a very important question for me to consider: "Am I now trying to win the approval of men, or of God?"

Many times in my life I have gotten caught up in seeking man's approval. It is so easy to get caught up in what others think and say about you. While it is important to be a good witness for Christ by my actions and deeds, I know the only opinion I need to concern myself with is God's. He sees me as His holy and dearly loved child. It is impossible to live my life trying to be all things to all people; therefore, I will keep my eyes fixed on God and live my life for an audience of one. I will seek to keep my heart pure before Him. I will be in constant prayer that He would reveal to me any wicked ways within me so that I can confess them before Him. I will trust Him to forgive me and lead me in ways of righteousness. When others seek to judge and condemn me I will listen for truths of things I need to improve upon, weed out untruths spoken out of emotion, and take it all to God and leave it with Him. I will forgive the other person for any hurt he has caused me and then put the incident behind me and move forward as a better person, not a bitter person. I only want God's approval.

Not only must we record key Scriptures on paper, we must also store them up in our heart so that they are with us at all times. Proverbs 3:1–4 says, "My son, do not forget my teaching, but keep my commands in your heart, for they will prolong your life many years and bring you prosperity. Let love and faithfulness never leave you; bind them around your neck, write them on the tablet of your heart. Then you will win favor and a good name in the sight of God and man." There have been times in my life when I have stored up many things in my heart, things like anger, hurt, disappointment, and resentment. I had to let God clean out the junk in my heart so that it could then be filled with His Word. A heart that is filled with God is a happy, content, and confident heart.

Plan Goals

I like it that the first two letters of the word *goal* spell *go*. That's exactly what our goals should do—put us in motion toward a positive direction. During my pregnancy with my first child, I gained fifty-five pounds. I wasn't very alarmed by this dramatic weight gain because I thought it would magically go away after I gave birth. Well, my baby didn't come out weighing fifty-five pounds. She weighed in at a mere seven pounds. I cried as I pulled and tugged, trying to put on my pre-pregnancy jeans. I couldn't get them above my knees. I stared at this strange body I had suddenly acquired. *What in the world has happened to me?* I wondered in disbelief. So, like many women before me, I went to my husband and asked him the dreaded question, "Honey, do I look fat?"

He squirmed, squinted, tilted his head, and tried to sound convincing as he sweetly replied, "No, dear." I reminded him that God commanded us not to lie, as I stormed away crying. He followed after me saying that he loved me and couldn't understand why I was so upset. Then he innocently and naively said something that stopped me dead in my tracks. "I think what you need is a goal. If you feel like you need to lose weight, why don't you go get certified to teach aerobics? I've never seen an overweight aerobics instructor."

That nearly sent me over the edge! After picking my jaw up off the floor, I decided to show him. I would go get certified to teach aerobics. This goal moved me from wishful thinking to positive action. I lost the weight, felt great, and actually enjoyed teaching aerobics.

Thomas Edison said, "The trouble with most people is that they quit before they start." Don't catch yourself saying, "I could never do that." You must believe, as Philippians 4:13 says, that with Christ it is possible, and visualize yourself reaching your goals.

I saw this played out recently when I attended a Carolina's Panther game with my friend Laura. Her husband, John, is one of the top-rated kickers in the NFL and plays for the Carolina Panthers. The game was in the last few seconds when John was summoned onto the field to attempt what would be a career record for him. The game was on the line. Make it and we win. Miss it and the game goes into overtime. With all eyes and cameras focused on him, John stepped onto the field. He looked up at the goal posts, and then down at the ball, swiftly approached the holder, drew back his leg and kicked with all his might. He split the uprights with a successful sixty-one-yard field goal. John knows what it means to set your sights on a goal. He saw the ball going through the goal posts before he ever drew back his leg to kick. How do you see yourself?

Many great men and women have failed before reaching their goals. Henry Ford forgot to put a reverse gear in his first car. Thomas Edison spent years and millions of dollars on an invention that never became much of anything. Probably one of the most amazing stories of perseverance is that of President Abraham Lincoln. He failed in business in 1831. He was defeated for the legislature in 1832 and failed in business again in 1833. In 1835 his fiancée died. He was defeated for Speaker of the Illinois house in 1838, and defeated for elector in 1840. Three of his four sons died before their nineteenth birthdays. He was defeated for Congress in 1843 and 1848, and for the Senate in 1855. He lost the race for vice president in 1856 and was defeated for the Senate again in 1858. Then, in 1860, Abraham Lincoln was elected President of the United States of America. President Abraham Lincoln said, "My great concern is not whether you have failed, but whether you are content with your failure." Do not fear failing, fear never trying. Let your goals be tangible reminders that you are not finished trying. Let them motivate you to persevere and to rise to new heights.

Outline Action Steps

These are the critical steps that must be taken in order for a goal to be reached. Action steps are practical, everyday choices that require obedience. You must decide at each critical step to take hold of your goal and choose to move toward it. Philippians 3:14 says, "I press on toward the goal to win the prize for which God has called me heavenward in Christ Jesus." Don't dwell on past failures and allow them to drag you down to defeat. Keep your eyes on your goal and press on. Norman P. Grubb said, "When the divine owner takes possession of a property, He has a twofold objective: intense cultivation and abounding fruitfulness." God wants to cultivate your life in order that you may produce fruit that brings Him glory.

When outlining your action steps, pray for wisdom before you list your action steps, pray for strength as you begin accomplishing your action steps, and thank God each time you meet one of your goals. Remember that your action steps should break down your goals into smaller steps that are specific and measurable. Under each of your goals, outline the action steps that must be accomplished if you are to meet that goal. Here are some action steps I listed for keeping my purpose in mind:

Goal: Develop a life plan that equips me to fulfill my purpose.
Action Steps:

- Spend time with God every day, praying and reading the Bible
- Journal my prayers and the life lessons God teaches me

- Find an accountability partner to review this Life Plan with once a month in order to help me stay on track
- Memorize fifty-two key scriptures
- Write a purpose statement that defines why I exist
- Finish this Life Plan

Please keep in mind that there will be days when you are tired of pressing on. But take heart. God wants you to succeed. Second Corinthians 4:16–18 says:

Therefore we do not lose heart. Though outwardly we are wasting away, yet inwardly we are being renewed day by day. For our light and momentary troubles are achieving for us an eternal glory that far outweighs them all. So we fix our eyes not on what is seen, but on what is unseen. For what is seen is temporary, but what is unseen is eternal.

It is worth it to keep going. Fix your eyes on Christ. Get down on your knees and ask Him to help you. Remember: The more we focus on Jesus, the less we focus on our problems. If He is our focus, everything else pales in comparison.

Set a Realistic Schedule

One Sunday my pastor put two jars on the podium. One had several rocks in it and the other was full of sand. He told us that the rocks represented the things in our lives that are truly important and the sand was everything else that we fill our calendars with. He showed us that if we took the jar with the sand already in it and tried to cram the rocks in on top of the sand, not very many rocks would fit. However, when he took the rocks and put them in the jar first, the sand poured in and around the rocks and it all fit.

My husband and I took this lesson to heart. We came home determined to put the "rocks" of our lives into our schedules and then put the other things in. We decided that we would hold each other accountable and meet every Sunday to plan out that week's schedule. So each week we schedule our rocks before anything else: time with God, each other, and our children; maintaining our home; and maintaining our health through exercise. Once we put these into our weekly schedule, we fill in the gaps with the action steps from our plans and a reasonable amount of other activities. Notice I used the word *reasonable*. Remember that saying no to some of the activities that clamor for our time can sometimes be the most positive answer. I also try to leave plenty of blank spaces to allow for spontaneity and the unexpected. While this procedure might seem rigid to some, I would encourage you that if I could learn to live by and actually like a schedule, anyone can! I'm amazed by how much more effectively I'm able to use my time. I've also found it's not really that I didn't have enough time but rather that I was not properly managing the time I had.

Once you've established a schedule you will be able to see how much time it will take you to complete your action steps. You can then determine a realistic completion date for most of your goals. Don't be discouraged if the completion date seems far away. Just keep busy by checking off those action steps and committing your projects to prayer. Remember, a book is written one word at a time. A race is won one step at a time. A life is lived one day at a time. A goal is met one small victory at a time.

Setting a realistic schedule is often the missing link for people in reaching their goals. Many people set goals but become discouraged when they take much longer to accomplish than they anticipated, so they wind up quitting. Then they establish a pattern of half-finished projects and a long list of excuses. Zig Ziglar says, "The saddest words in the English language are 'If only.'" Breaking your goals down into time-sensitive action steps and daily disciplines can break this pattern and get you back on track toward meeting your goals and realizing your dreams.

Examine Your Progress

Examining your progress is the most exciting part of this whole process. Remember preparing for exams when you were in school? You made the effort to take good notes. You read the required reading.

You worked hard, studied for the big test, took the test, and walked out feeling good. You could hardly wait to see your grade. A couple of days later, the grades were posted and you made an A. Then you felt great and you couldn't wait for the report card to be sent home. That's your reward. It's your moment of victory. Don't miss it. Make sure you take the time to examine your progress and celebrate each of your victories.

Just as a report card grade helps motivate students to learn, you may need prizes to give you incentive. People love prizes. They are great motivators. Have you ever noticed at the fair how much money people are willing to throw away in hopes of winning that silly little stuffed animal? Why? Because, people love to win prizes.

I love to win prizes. When I was in college, I worked at an Italian restaurant as a waitress. I was a good waitress until the day I was transformed into a great waitress. The manager decided he wanted to sell more appetizers, so he developed a contest. Whoever sold the most appetizers during the next month would win a portable CD player. Well, I became the appetizer queen. I bet I still hold the record to this day. You see, it wasn't selling the most appetizers that got me motivated; it was the thrill of winning the prize. Think of some prizes that would motivate you and start enjoying the sweet taste of victory.

Another great motivator is an accountability partner. There is nothing that makes a victory sweeter than when you have a friend to share it with. I highly recommend finding an accountability partner to help you examine your progress. An accountability partner can spur you on when you're ready to quit, pick you up and dust you off when you stumble, praise you when you've reached a certain milestone, and celebrate with you at the finish line. If you don't have an accountability partner, ask God to bring to mind the right person to ask. Make sure this person is encouraging, clearly understands your vision, and is bold enough to hold you accountable.

Here are some questions you might find helpful when you are examining your progress.

- Am I glorifying God in this area of my life?
- Am I working toward fulfilling my purpose in this area? How?

- How is my prayer life? Am I regularly praying for this area of my life?
- What have I recently learned from God's Word about this area of my life?
- What Scripture have I memorized to help me in this area?
- What action steps have I completed to help me move closer toward meeting some of my goals for this area?
- What goal or goals have I met?
- Am I managing my schedule well? Am I putting the "rocks" of my life first? Are there activities I need to eliminate from my schedule?
- Who do I have to hold me accountable in this area of my life?
- Am I seeing positive life changes from having a Life Plan? If yes, list some of those here. If no, write out why not.

If you have *The Life Planning Journal for Women,* you will notice there is enough room in your journal to examine your progress once a month for one year. If you are making your own journal, I would encourage you to transfer the questions listed above into this section of your journal. I would also encourage you to examine your progress once a month in all Seven Principles.

Finally, each time you reach a milestone or meet one of your goals, record it in some way. In my home we have a "You Are Special" red plate that we pull out each time one of us has one of those "way to go" days. We take a picture of the person and then put the picture in a special red scrapbook. I journal next to the picture the accomplishment we were celebrating. I would encourage you to keep a success journal of some kind for you and your family. Then, on those "no-good, rotten, I'm having a bad hair and attitude" days, you can pull out your journal and remind yourself how very thankful you should be and how very special you really are. This works great with adults and kids alike!

You will find it helpful to refer back to this chapter when completing Section 2, Parts 10–16 in your *Life Planning Journal for Women.* Re-

member: We will be using the P.U.R.P.O.S.E. model to help structure the remainder of our Life Plan.

WORKING ON YOUR JOURNAL

Take time to work on Section 2, Part 9, of your journal. If you have *The Life Planning Journal for Women*, turn there now. (The questions listed below are already included in the journal itself.) If you are making your own journal, transfer the questions below to your journal and spend some time recording your answers. Then remember to complete each step of the P.U.R.P.O.S.E. model described in chapter 9.

Now that we have defined the components for finding P.U.R.P.O.S.E., we are ready to start the exciting application of this material. So let's go on to chapter 10, "The Holy Pursuit: Finding My Purpose as a Child of God." There we will focus on Principle #1: *The Proverbs 31 woman reveres Jesus Christ as Lord of her life and pursues an ongoing, personal relationship with Him.*

QUESTIONS TO CONSIDER IN YOUR JOURNAL

1. Read Acts 5:38–39. Journal your thoughts.
2. Why is prayer going to be so very important as you develop your Life Plan?
3. What does God promise us in Jeremiah 29:11? Journal how this verse encourages you.
4. Read and record Proverbs 16:3 here.
5. What is the world's definition of success?
6. What is God's definition of success?
7. How do we invite God to become intimately involved in our lives?
8. Read and record Romans 12:2.
9. How can you know what God's will is?

10. Read Philippians 3:14. Are you dwelling on past failures or are you pressing on as this verse instructs? Journal your thoughts.

11. What is often the missing link for people in reaching their goals?

12. What qualities should you look for when looking for an accountability partner?

13. Write down the names of a couple of people you would like to start praying about concerning whether God would have one of them be your accountability partner.

Chapter Ten

THE HOLY PURSUIT: FINDING MY PURPOSE AS A CHILD OF GOD

PRINCIPLE #1: The Proverbs 31 woman reveres Jesus Christ as Lord of her life and pursues an ongoing, personal relationship with Him.

Of all the relationships in my life, my relationship with Jesus is of paramount importance. John 14:27 says, "Peace I leave with you; my peace I give you. I do not give to you as the world gives. Do not let your hearts be troubled and do not be afraid." The heart of every person longs for peace. People may think they long for money, success, fame, comfort, power, and many other things the world tries to tell us will bring us happiness. However, world-based happiness fades and can be quickly lost. I've found the only lasting happiness comes from a life filled with the peace of God.

In order to explore this more completely I want us to examine some key components to the peace of God that will enable us to live out Principle #1. We must first understand that Jesus is the only right price for our salvation. Then we will seek to understand how to pursue an ongoing and personal relationship with Him through understanding how to fear Him and find His joy. This will be an exciting chapter that will conclude with a thought-provoking section on finding your purpose as a child of God. At the conclusion of the chapter, we'll turn to Section 2, Part 10, of our journals (either the journal you are making or *The Life Planning Journal for Women*) and work on the next part of our Life Plan.

The Right Price

My heart raced with excitement as we approached the tall gray-haired man with the large black book. Everyone standing in line was focused on what they would say when it was finally his turn. My turn came and went and I wondered with great anticipation if my name was one of the few written in the man's book. I filed into the row of seats my group was directed toward, took my seat, and waited.

Suddenly, huge spotlights flashed on and their beams started turning somersaults all around us. Large cameras came to life as the crowd was directed to cheer and show our excitement to be there. I held my breath as the first four names were called. My heart leapt as I heard my first name, only to sink when it was called with the wrong last name. A game was played, then a commercial, and then it was time for another name. "Lysa TerKeurst come on down! You're the next contestant on *The Price Is Right!*" I screamed, jumped up and down, hugged half the people on my row, and ran to my place in Contestants' Row.

Now I wish I could tell you how I impressed the nation with my great bidding abilities and all about the fabulous prizes I won. Sorry to disappoint you, but I and all my excitement stayed right there on Contestants' Row. However, I did walk away with some nice parting gifts—and even better than those was the life lesson God taught me.

One day we all will stand in line with great excitement as we approach a tall figure with a large book—and we all will want our names to be written there. However, nothing we say or do or have done in the past will be enough to win us a spot in that book. The names written there are all the people who have at some time surrendered their life to God and accepted Jesus Christ as their personal Lord and Savior. And on that day we will not be able to stand as we approach the Almighty, for it is written that every knee shall bow and every tongue shall confess that He is Lord. Each one of us will desire with every ounce of his being to be called and then ushered into the glory of our Father's presence. And then there are our treasures. The mansion prepared just for us on a street paved with gold. The crowns of glory we will be able to place at the foot of our Father. The loved ones we have grieved that have been awaiting our reunion. And best of all, Jesus. We will be able to see Him in all His glory and talk to Him face-to-face.

Yes, it was exciting to be on *The Price Is Right*, but like everything else in this world the thrill was temporary and the glory fleeting. The only things lasting and eternal are found through our relationship with Jesus—the One who is the only "right price." He has paid the price for our sins so that we may spend eternity in heaven. He has given us the amazing privilege to come to Him personally at any time and talk about anything and everything. I often think about how honored I'd be if the president of the United States called and said that he would like to spend an hour in conversation with me. I'd do whatever it took to rearrange my schedule and eliminate competing distractions. Yet, my Lord desires this time with me every day, and I find myself at times barely able to squeeze Him in. Do you find this to be true in your life?[1]

The Fear of the Lord

The Proverbs 31 woman cannot afford not to spend time with God. He is her number one priority. The Scriptures tell us that she fears the Lord. This is not an afraid-of-God fear. This is a reverent fear. She fears not spending time with Him, so she gets up early and calls upon Him. She knows His voice because she has heard it many times. She dedicates all she has and all she is to Him. She lets Him direct her steps and set her schedule. Her mind has been transformed to follow after Christ's pattern for life, and His Word is stored up in her heart.

Do you desire to have this kind of relationship with the Father? I know I do. I know that ultimately my relationship with God is the purpose for which I was created. Yes, God has plans for me to do things. Yes, God has purposes for me to fulfill. But all of this would be for nothing if I miss out on the divine reason for my existence—and that is to fellowship with, worship, and, yes, fear the Father.

Isaiah 33:6 says, "He will be the sure foundation for your times, a rich store of salvation and wisdom and knowledge; the fear of the Lord is the key to this treasure." This verse is instructing us that to fear the Lord means to open up a treasure of salvation, wisdom, and knowledge. To fear the Lord means to revere Him and seek Him. So how do we do this? Psalm 34:11–14 says, "Come, my children, listen to me; I will teach you the fear of the Lord. Whoever of you loves life and desires to see many good days, keep your tongue from evil and your lips from speaking lies. Turn from evil and do good; seek peace and pursue it."

Proverbs 31 tells us that a woman who fears the Lord is to be praised. This is why the Proverbs 31 woman reveres Jesus Christ as Lord of her life. Then, and only then, will we be able to love life and see many good days. Our goal in life should not be to merely survive, but rather thrive as we seek the one that created us and let Him guide us to our purpose.

The Joy of the Lord

As I sit down to write this section on joy, I can't help but laugh at myself; otherwise, I might cry. I had such grand plans today. While my older two daughters were off at school and my youngest went down for her nap, I had planned to write some long overdue thank-you notes, wash a couple loads of laundry, and write about joy. I had no idea that Satan himself was going to rear his ugly head in the form of an overflowed washing machine and a computer with a mind of its own. Needless to say the thank-yous once again didn't get done, I'm still behind on my laundry, the baby will be waking up any minute now, and here I sit in front of a computer that no matter how I beg it to cooperate couldn't care less about my feelings.

The psalmist says, "This is the day that the Lord has made; let us rejoice and be glad in it." This passage does not say as long as everything is zippidy-do-dah have a wonderful day. No, it says *this* day is a gift from God, and no matter what happens we can choose to be thankful for it and find the joy God intended for us today.

A friend of mine has this verse beautifully painted on one of her kitchen walls. I need that kind of reminder, especially on days like today where everywhere I turn something tries to steal my joy. You see, if I can't rejoice and be glad today I will never rejoice and be glad. I will waste the joyous opportunities of today waiting for tomorrows that may or may not ever come. If I wait until life slows down, the sun comes back, the kids are older and less demanding, I lose some weight, my husband gets that raise, then I'll spend my life waiting rather than living and being glad.

The joys of life are found in and amongst life itself. Yes, life is full of frustrations, disappointments, pain, and suffering; but no matter what we are facing, having an attitude of joy will allow us to find the good that God promises us is there. If an oyster can make a pearl out of an irritating grain of sand, just think of what you could do if in every situation you chose to rejoice and be glad rather than succumbing to the flesh's natural response.

Will you now suddenly be able to find joy in all situations as a result of reading and heeding this advice? Probably not, but maybe it will cause you to stop and think about ways to rediscover joy in your life. Maybe it will cause you to choose to make pearls out of the irritations that will inevitably try to steal your joy today. Pray and ask God to help restore the joy that He intends for you to have. Invite Jesus to teach you through all circumstances how to be more like Him. Let your heart be sensitive to the Holy Spirit's conviction when your joy starts to slip away. Then the next time you feel life getting you down, remember that it takes forty-three muscles to frown and only seventeen to smile.

Proverbs 15:15 (TLB) says, "When a man is gloomy, everything seems to go wrong; when he is cheerful, everything seems right!" This sounds pretty close to another saying I've heard: "If mama ain't happy, ain't nobody happy." How true that is. The woman of a house has the unique responsibility to set the tone of her home much like a thermostat sets the temperature. When I'm having a good day, my home is full of love and laughter. However, on those not-so-good days, bad attitudes seem to abound.

So how do we find joy in the middle of both life's ups and life's downs? Nehemiah 8:10 says, "The joy of the Lord is your strength."

When I was a little girl, I remember my Sunday school teacher taught us a very simple but profound truth about joy. She said to find joy you must put Jesus first, others next, and yourself third. When the order of your life is *Jesus, Others, Yourself*, you can't help but find JOY. There is a lot of truth to that simple childhood acronym. When seeking to find your purpose as a child of God, you must remember that the fear of the Lord will lead you to salvation, wisdom, and knowledge, and the joy of the Lord will be the strength that will keep you going.

Your Purpose as a Child of God

I really don't like to wait. I don't like waiting in line at the grocery store while my kids use every trick in the book to get me to buy the candy strategically placed at their eye level. I don't like waiting in the pediatrician's office while every germ known to mankind bombards my children. I don't like waiting to be seated at a restaurant or standing in line for the restroom. But the one that gets me the most is waiting in traffic—especially construction traffic.

Once, when one of the main roads leading to my home was repaved, I was stuck in a long, slow-moving line. I had no choice but to wait. Frustration mounted as I realized they were only letting a few cars through at a time that had to be led off the road, around equipment, through a grassy area, and then back on the road. That lead truck then had to take the time to turn around and lead cars going in the opposite direction through the same maze. I thought about being a rebel and four-wheeling my minivan through the big open field to my left, thus avoiding the wait and giving all the other motorists a little comic relief while they waited. However, my conscience kicked in, and coupled with the fact that I have a Proverbs 31 bumper sticker on the rear of my van, I decided to stay put.

My turn finally came fifteen minutes later. When the lead truck turned to guide my group through the construction I saw for the first time a sign hanging on his tailgate that read, "Pilot Vehicle, Follow Me." The words instantly touched something in my heart. They reminded me of my Savior calling me to let Him be the pilot vehicle for my life and simply follow Him. As my van bumped and jiggled through the rough terrain I suddenly became so thankful for this pilot vehicle and realized the importance of waiting to let him lead me in his timing, slow as it was, because his was the best route to the other side. Tears came to my eyes as my thoughts again turned to Jesus. He wants to lead us through the best routes in life but we must be willing to follow and patiently wait for His timing.

The world is full of big open fields to the right and to the left of God's narrow way that seem so much better, quicker, and even easier to the human eye. How easily we can be deceived and led astray because we don't realize the dangers of going our own way. We want to avoid the construction stops in life, and yet they are just where God does some of the most life-changing work on us. We want to avoid waiting, and yet this is where we are called to draw near to God, trust in His love, and realize that only His timing is perfect.

Let me encourage you to be thankful for whatever construction is interrupting your life right now and encourage you to let Jesus be your pilot vehicle through this time. Remember, God never promised us the easiest, most timely route. He promised the *best* route. Jesus said, "I am the light of the world. Whoever follows me will never walk in darkness, but will have the light of life" (John 8:12). In seeking to understand your purpose as a child of God, it is vital to keep your eyes fixed on your pilot vehicle. He knows where you need to go and what you need to do once you get there. He has already planned and purposed divine appointments for you at each bend in your life's road. Corrie ten Boom said, "Every experience God gives us, every person He puts in our lives is the perfect preparation for the future that only He can see."

The key to a successful journey in your search for your purpose as a child of God is having enough fear of the Lord to keep your eyes fixed on Him, balanced with the joy of the Lord that will assure you that you're never alone. He is right there cheering you on in the good times, wiping your tears during times of sorrow, and carrying you when you get weary. He loves you. Oh my, how the Father loves you.

WORKING ON YOUR JOURNAL

Take time to work on Section 2, Part 10, of your journal. If you have The Life Planning Journal for Women, turn there now. (The questions listed below are already included in the journal itself.) If you are making your own journal, transfer the questions below to your journal and spend some time recording your answers. Then remember to complete each step of the P.U.R.P.O.S.E. model described in chapter 9.

Once you complete this section of your journal, continue your reading with chapter 11, "Making the Most of My Marriage: Finding My Purpose as a Wife."

QUESTIONS TO CONSIDER IN YOUR JOURNAL

1. Do you struggle at times with pursuing an ongoing relationship with Jesus?

2. Why do the Scriptures say the Proverbs 31 woman fears the Lord?

3. Read Isaiah 33:6 and record it.

4. Where are the joys of life found?

5. Read Nehemiah 8:10 and record it.

6. Where do we draw our strength from?

7. Why should we not try to avoid the construction stops in life?

8. What should we do while waiting on God?

9. Read John 8:12 and record it.

10. What three divine appointments have you had that have had the most monumental effects on your life? Write about them.

11. What is the key to a successful journey in searching for your purpose as a child of God?

Note

1. The section "The Right Price" was adapted from "My Name Was Called," by Lysa TerKeurst, in *The Best of* the Proverbs 31 Ministry (Charlotte, N.C.: The Proverbs 31 Ministry, 1999), 15–16. Used by permission of the author.

Chapter Eleven

MAKING THE MOST OF MY MARRIAGE: FINDING MY PURPOSE AS A WIFE

PRINCIPLE #2: The Proverbs 31 woman loves,
honors and respects her husband as head of the home.

I remember as a young woman gazing at the stars one beautiful summer night praying for a husband. My heart ached for someone to love, my arms for someone to hold, and my eyes to see the wonderful gift God was preparing for me. I remember wondering what he would look like, what new last name he would give me, and how long would it be before our paths would cross. Soon after that night, I got a call from my friend Dean informing me that he played golf that day with the man I was going to marry. Dean was right. Less than a year later, I was enjoying those beautiful stars with a man, my man, my husband.

There were times that first year that I thanked God from the bottom of my heart for making all my dreams come true. Then there were those times where I gave God a list of all the things He needed to fix in this man of mine. I knew he was a gift, but sometimes I wished I could wrap him up in brown paper and stick a "Return to Sender" label on him. (And I can assure you that he felt the same about me!) Over the years God has taught us both how to appreciate and accept one another, love and forgive one another, and serve and sacrifice for one another. The most important word in that previous sentence is *God*. He designed marriage. So if we want ours to be the best it can be, we must seek to do things His way.

As we work on the marriage section of our Life Plans, we must first understand God's design for marriage; learn how to become a woman of love; discover creative ways to love, honor, and respect our husband; and finally be challenged to fulfill our purpose as a wife. That's what this chapter is all about. I hope you find little nuggets of truth, wisdom, and encouragement throughout that will make you want to go grab that man of yours, look him squarely in the eyes, and tell him there's a new girl in town that's just madly in love with him—his wife!

Seeking God's Design for Marriage

It's amazing what God can teach us through little children. I learned a most important lesson one day while teaching children's church. I told the children that we were going to memorize a Bible verse—and then after they could recite their verse, they would be rewarded with a snack. One little boy was so excited about getting his snack that he wanted to be the first to try. The verse was "Jesus came to seek and save that which was lost." As little Cameron stood in front of the class, he twisted his face, stuffed his hands deep into his pants pockets, and proudly blurted out, "Jesus came . . . to save us . . . and He got lost." I did not have the heart to correct him so I just chuckled and handed him his snack.

Later as I recounted this story to his parents, the thought struck me that while Jesus never gets lost, Cameron's version did have a lot of truth to it. Many of us try to handle by ourselves the struggles we face in life. This seems especially true in marriages. It's as if Jesus seeks to help us improve our marriage, but we tell Him to get lost. We tell Him to get lost when He instructs wives in Ephesians 5:22 to submit and willingly let their husbands be the leaders of their homes. We'd rather not listen to His advice in Proverbs 19:13 about not being quarrelsome lest we become like a leaky faucet. We are quick to forget the last half of Ephesians 5:33 where we are told to respect our husbands. Sometimes we'd rather be our huband's "*nagavator*" through the journey of life rather than trusting God to guide his steps. First Peter 3:1–2 says, "Wives, in the same way be submissive to your husbands so that, if any of them do not believe the word, they may be won over without words by the behavior of their wives, when they see the purity and reverence of your lives." I think that verse says it all.

The men are not off the hook here, either. They would rather put aside Ephesians 5:25, which tells them they are supposed to love us as much as Christ loves the church, even to the point of dying for us. When things get tense at home, they are sometimes quick to respond harshly even though Colossians 3:19 instructs otherwise.

Now don't get me wrong, my husband and I are just as guilty of this as anyone. Sometimes I blow it. I mean I really blow it. You see, occasionally this other woman—my husband affectionately calls her Sabrina—kidnaps me and takes my place as my husband's wife. She has a bad attitude and through her stinky morning breath she voices her opinions in the most unkind and harsh ways. She is easily offended, holds a grudge, and swears to get even as she accidentally on purpose oversalts his eggs. She is clothed with a sour expression on her face and because she can't find her distaff she grasps a wooden spoon and strikes a martyr's pose. She eats the bread of idleness for breakfast as she stews about all *he* has done wrong today. What really sends her over the edge is when she hears her husband whisper as he leaves for work, "Many women do crazy things, but you surpass them all!"

OK. I admit it isn't Sabrina, it is me—the Proverbs 31 woman in her not-so-finest hour. Well, we all fail and fall short. That's why I'm so glad there is one word that never appears in Proverbs 31—the word *perfect*. The goal should not be to be a perfect wife and mother but to be a woman who is not afraid to turn to the One who *is* perfect and seek His face when she has fallen flat on hers. So I pushed aside my bread of idleness and picked up the Word of God, and what I found is that God is a God of do-overs. According to Philippians 1:6, "He who began a good work in you will carry it on to completion." What God requires of me is to be willing to walk humbly with Him every day and allow

Him to mold and shape me into the wife my husband needs. When I do this my husband is much more willing to love me the way I long to be loved. Bill Gillham, in The Roles [Marriage] Seminar, summed it up when he said, "How can your husband carry you around on a silver platter if you're never even willing to climb up on the plate?"

A Woman of Love

Do you remember in grade school when your definition of love boiled down to a simple question, "Will you go with me? Check either yes or no." Then in high school you thought you knew everything about love. Love was writing your first name with your boyfriend's last name over and over while you were pretending to take notes in history class. It was sleeping with the phone so as not to miss your loved one's call. It was having a date to prom where you dressed like a princess and your Prince Charming traded his faded jeans for a stunning tuxedo. Finally, you moved past all the puppy love stuff and into real love that came complete with a ring, a bouquet, a kiss, and a lifetime promise. Just when you thought you had love all figured out, real life struck. Somewhere between the mound of bills and the children clamoring for your attention, you realized you might need a little help understanding what true love really is. Well, I say, when in doubt go back and read the owner's manual. In this case, that would be the Bible—1 Corinthians 13:4–8.

Love is patient, love is kind. It does not envy, it does not boast, it is not proud. —1 Corinthians 13:4

My husband needs a "completer" not a "complainer." He needs me to come along beside him in the areas where he is weak and help him, not hinder him. In Genesis 2:18 the Lord says, "'It is not good for the man to be alone. I will make a helper suitable for him.'" God expects me to complete my husband by helping him become the man God intends for him to be. I have been given that awesome responsibility. It's much easier to sit back and complain about areas in which my husband is weak, but that is not God's plan. What *is* His plan is for a woman's husband to have "full confidence in her . . . [as] she brings him good, not harm, all the days of her life" (Proverbs 31:11–12).

The Proverbs 31 woman helped her husband become a well-respected leader in his community. I can help my husband become all that God has intended him to be by following the Bible's definition of love. I can be patient with his progress, give kind words of encouragement, never envy his successes nor boast of my involvement. I can give out of a humble heart. What could your husband become if you came alongside him as God intended you to?

It is not rude, it is not self-seeking, it is not easily angered, it keeps no record of wrongs.
—1 Corinthians 13:5

This part seems to trip me up in my pursuit of becoming a woman of true "love" every time. If I make a concerted effort to bite my tongue, most of the time I can handle not being rude or self-seeking. The easily angered part only seems to trip me up during that one week of the month where I am stricken with "Princess Must Scream" disorder: P.M.S. However, the keeping no record of wrongs is extremely difficult. I have been known to forget where I put my purse, forget where I've parked my car, and forget all kinds of appointments—but seldom do I forget the wrongs of my husband. Keeping no record of wrongs means to choose to forgive and refuse to use past wrongs as ammunition during the next disagreement. This is hard to do, but if we want to discover the kind of love God intended for us to have in our marriages, we must follow His instructions completely.

Love does not delight in evil but rejoices with the truth.
—1 Corinthians 13:6

Jesus says in John 8:31–32, "If you hold to my teaching, you are really my disciples. Then you will know the truth, and the truth will set you free." There are three truths you will discover in holding to God's Word and letting God be in the center of your relationship.

1. *You are and forever will be a holy and dearly loved child of God, and the same is true of your husband.* Look at your husband through God's eyes and your whole perception will change. Yes, he has flaws, but who doesn't? Focus on all his many God-given strengths and make it a habit to praise and honor him often.

2. *Fixing someone else is an impossible task.* Yet many times when a marriage starts struggling, one partner decides his or her spouse needs to be "fixed." But all of my efforts to fix my husband just made him pull away from me. I learned that if things were going to get better I had to get my focus off of Art and let God change me.

3. *Harboring resentment will do nothing but damage your marriage.* Make it a point to forgive your husband. Remember the beauty of forgiveness is that it releases you from the bondage of unforgiveness. There may be some things God needs to deal with in your husband, but leave those things to God and live in the freedom that comes from forgiving as Christ forgives you. Remember that Ephesians 6 teaches us that our mate is not our enemy—Satan is.[1]

It always protects, always trusts, always hopes, always perseveres. Love never fails.

—1 Corinthians 13:7–8a

We should always persevere in our marriages. Too many people are giving up on one of God's greatest gifts—marriage. It is not time to give up. It is time to get on our faces before God and seek Him. I need to protect my marriage by seeking to understand my husband's needs and meeting them to the best of my ability.

However, in order to meet the needs of another person, you've got to first understand what his/her needs are! According to Willard Harley in his book *His Needs, Her Needs,* the five greatest needs for a man are (1) sexual fulfillment, (2) recreational companionship, (3) an attractive spouse, (4) domestic support, and (5) admiration and respect.[2] It is important to talk with your husband and ask him specifically what his needs are. Then do all you can to protect your marriage, trust your husband, keep hope alive, and persevere, knowing that true love never fails.

Creative Ways to Love, Honor, and Respect Your Husband

One day I was running with my husband and feeling pretty good about meeting one of his greatest needs—recreational companionship.

Suddenly, thoughts of resentment started to creep in as I thought about all that I wished my husband would do to meet *my* needs. Because my husband is not a mind reader, I knew I needed to communicate my desires to him if there was any hope at all of his doing what I desired. However, telling him what I wanted would defeat the purpose. I wanted to be surprised and excited that he thought enough of me to plan special things on his own. I started praying and asking God to miraculously plant creative thoughts into the mind of my husband. Instead, God planted a creative thought in my mind. Thus, the birth of the "Love Jar" concept.

As soon as we returned from running, I found two empty jars and labeled them "Lysa's love jar" and "Art's love jar." I put five slips of paper in mine and five in his. I put a big smile on my face, and approached my hunk of love with the jars. I instructed him to write something on each of his papers that would speak love to him. I did the same on the papers in my jar. I told him for the next five weeks we would pick one thing out of each other's jars and make a point to do whatever was written on it. I just knew his papers would say: sex, sex, sex. But, you'll never guess what the first slip I pulled out said: make him a fruit salad! He even listed out the fruit he wanted in his salad: kiwi, strawberries, cantaloupe, grapes, and watermelon. (Isn't my husband precious.) I was stunned. I would have never guessed in a million years that a fruit salad would speak volumes of love to my man. He pulled out the slip of paper that read, "Take me shopping and let me give you lots of gift ideas for future special occasions." I have since made many fruit salads and he has taken me on many shopping adventures.

Learning how to creatively meet our spouse's needs and expectations will help keep the relationship alive, fun, and exciting. Just in case you are running a little short on creativity, I've included a list written by my friend Bonita Lillie and originally printed in the newsletter *The Proverbs 31 Woman*.[3]

1. Learn your mate's love language. (For more information, see Gary Chapman's book *The Five Love Languages* [Chicago: Moody, 1992, 1995]).
2. Never forget his love language and speak it often.
3. Read 1 Corinthians 13:4–8 and live it.

4. Treat your spouse to an old-fashioned foot washing.

5. Give him a body massage and, as you do, pray aloud for him.

6. Leave an intimate note on his pillow that lets him know he is a great lover.

7. Create an atmosphere of peace in the home, especially when he arrives home from work.

8. Pray for his life and success daily.

9. Do a chore that is supposed to be his responsibility.

10. Help him make and maintain male friendships by allowing him time away with the boys.

11. When he has had an especially hard day or on the day he pays the bills, romance him that evening.

12. Praise him in public.

13. Praise him to your parents and in-laws.

14. Save money in a jar and buy him something he really wants.

15. After the kids are in bed, slow dance by candlelight or firelight.

16. Build him up in the eyes of your children. Make him their greatest hero.

17. Handle small irritations for him, such as junk mail and getting things fixed around the house.

18. When he asks you to do something, do it.

19. Support his life ambitions in both word and deed.

20. Make sure he always has clean underwear.

21. If he's agreeable, take up a new hobby or interest together or share those you already have.

22. Be quick to say I'm sorry and even quicker to forgive.

23. Don't complain.

24. Be a woman he can trust. Don't share more than you should with others.

25. Don't depend on him to meet all your needs. Make friends with other women.

26. When he arrives home from work, allow him some quiet time and then discuss his day before you talk about yours.

27. Maintain your health and beauty. Don't be a sight for sore eyes.

28. Avoid jealousy. Trust him.

29. Make a cassette tape of inspiring words and thoughts (yours or those from another source) that he can play on the way to and from work.

30. Play a funny, but safe, practical joke on him to add humor to your life.

31. Pray for his weaknesses and praise his strengths.

32. Exercise together.

33. Keep the bedroom exciting.

34. Put your husband before your children and make sure he knows that he will always hold that place.

35. Plan regular date nights. Be creative and do different things.

36. Have a special treat sent to his workplace, such as a cookie that says, "I love you."

37. Give him a nickname that only the two of you know.

38. Spend time talking about your dating days and what first attracted you to him. When you are tempted to think of him in a negative light, remind yourself of these things.

39. Always express thankfulness for all he does for your family, whether it be big or small.

40. Use physical affection often—a hand on the shoulder, a neck rub, a stroke on the cheek, a pat on the rear, etc.

41. The next time you are tempted to usurp his authority, don't.

42. Avoid pointing out his mistakes. No matter how many mistakes he has made in the past, believe for the best this time.

43. Surround yourself with friends who want to see your marriage last, and listen to them. Stay clear of those who point out your husband's faults.

44. Speak kindly and watch the tone of your voice.

45. Be there in his hour of need.

46. Be content with what you have, not always demanding more.

47. Be slow to speak and quick to listen.

48. Drop an encouraging note or Scripture verse into his lunch or briefcase.

49. Always celebrate your anniversary in some way.

50. On each anniversary remember old times and plan for the future.

51. Display your wedding pictures as well as any awards he may have won.

52. Keep the house reasonably tidy.

53. Give him the benefit of the doubt.

54. Treat him with respect, and teach the children to do the same.

55. Keep your promises.

56. Let him sleep in occasionally and serve him his favorite breakfast in bed.

57. Begin each day with a hug. End each night with a kiss.

58. On your anniversary or on Valentine's Day send him a love note via the classifieds in the paper.

59. Be thankful for your husband. Many people don't have what you have, so don't take him for granted.

60. Add to this list continually.

Your Purpose as a Wife

In Colossians 3 we see a beautiful set of guidelines for holy living. I know that if I can follow the Master's instructions here, I will fulfill my purpose as a wife. It instructs me to set my heart and mind on things above and not the earthly things of sexual immorality, impurity, lust, evil desires, and greed. I must also rid myself of anger, rage, malice, slander, and filthy language. I must never lie to my husband and must always look at him as a beautiful child of the Almighty Creator. We are equal partners with different roles. While God has called my husband to be the head of the home, He's called me to be the heart of the home. I am responsible to embrace the role of the wife and clothe myself with compassion, kindness, humility, gentleness, and patience. I must seek to bear my husband's burdens with him and always forgive him as Christ forgives me. I must always let the peace of Christ rule in my heart and be thankful. Above all else, I must love and let this virtue bind us together in perfect unity.

I pray that this chapter has inspired you to take a fresh look at your marriage and that you now seek to fulfill your purpose as a wife with a renewed excitement. I like to compare this marriage adventure to Christopher Columbus discovering America. There were times when he faced rough seas, times when many of his crew tried to get him to turn back, times when things happened that drew him off course, but if you read his journal, you'll see that he just kept writing, "Sailed on."

That's what our marriage journal needs to read—we sail on and never give up on our pursuit of discovering the marital fulfillment God intends for us. Then we, like Columbus, will make a great discovery!

WORKING ON YOUR JOURNAL

Take time to work on Section 2, Part 11, of your journal. If you have *The Life Planning Journal for Women,* turn there now. (The questions listed below are already included in the journal itself.) If you are making your own journal, transfer the questions below to your journal and spend some time recording your answers. Then remember to complete each step of the P.U.R.P.O.S.E. model described in chapter 9.

Once you complete this section of your journal, continue your reading with chapter 12, "The High Calling of Motherhood: Finding My Purpose as a Mother."

QUESTIONS TO CONSIDER IN YOUR JOURNAL

1. Read Ephesians 5:22–33 and record the verses.

2. What does God expect from you as a wife?

3. What does Proverbs 19:13 warn us not to be? Have you sprung any leaks lately?

4. Who is able to shape and mold you into the wife your husband needs?

5. Read Philippians 1:6 and record it.

6. Who will carry out His good work in you?

7. Read and record Genesis 2:18.

8. Have you caught yourself being more of a "complainer" than a "completer"? What are some ways you can be a suitable helper for your husband?

9. Read 1 Corinthians 13:4–8. List the characteristics of love as described in this passage. Put a star by the ones you do well and circle the ones you need to work on.

10. Write a commitment to pursue God's definition of love in your marriage.

11. List the five greatest needs of a man. Beside each write two things you could do to better meet his needs. (You can use the list of creative ideas from the book or make up your own.)

12. Pull out your schedule and write these special "to dos" in. Put a check mark here when you have scheduled them.

Notes

1. Adapted from "Putting Your Marriage on the Right Track, by Lysa TerKerurst, in *The Best of the Proverbs 31 Ministry: Encourage and Inspiration for Women* (Charlotte, N.C.: The Proverbs 31 Ministry, 1999), 63–64. Used by permission of the author.

2. Willard F. Harley Jr., *His Needs, Her Needs* (Grand Rapids: Revell, 1988).

3. Bonita Lillie, "More Than 50 Ways to Love Your Lover," in *The Best of the Proverbs 31 Ministry*, 87–90. Used by permission of the author.

Chapter Twelve

THE HIGH CALLING OF MOTHERHOOD: FINDING MY PURPOSE AS A MOTHER

PRINCIPLE #3: The Proverbs 31 woman nurtures her children and believes that motherhood is a high calling with the responsibility of shaping and molding the children who will one day define who we are as a community and nation.

Now that we have covered our relationships with God and our husband, with this chapter we will venture into the heart of motherhood. What an amazing responsibility God entrusts to us mothers. He gives us a chance to help shape and mold little people into magnificent legacies of love. While in some ways we must hold onto them tightly, in other ways we are in the process of letting go, from the moment the umbilical cord is cut. The peace that can be found throughout all of the holding on and letting go is through our trust in God.

In Isaiah 49:16a God says, "'See, I have engraved you on the palms of my hands.'" You see, moms, there will be times in life where we will have to trust God to hold onto our kids. And hold onto them He does! He holds them so tightly that they leave lasting impressions engraved into the palms of His hands. I learned this lesson when we almost lost our second child, Ashley. I remember standing in the hospital crying out to the Lord, pleading for Him to save my baby. My husband gently cupped my face in his hands and said, "Lysa, she is God's child first. If He chooses to save her or if He chooses to take her, you've got to be willing to give her to Him." I've never forgotten that conversation because it was so pivotal for me.

God did choose to spare Ashley and I am so very grateful. But just six years earlier I was in another hospital room pleading for the life of my one-year-old sister, and God chose to take her. We must know that our children are His first and into His care we must entrust them daily. It also gave me a fresh dose of perspective concerning whom I have been given to raise and train. He has given me His child. Oh, her hands may be shaped like mine and she may have her daddy's eyes, but she has a soul that belongs to the Master. May we find great purpose in mothering God's little people. May we give them good examples to follow, lead them in the ways everlasting, and always trust God to hold onto them tightly. Follow me now as we explore the high calling of motherhood, seek to make the most of the toughest job we'll ever love, discover how to develop a legacy of love, and examine our purpose as mothers.

The High Calling

OK. I have a confession to make. There are days when I lose my joy in this adventure known as motherhood. But on those trying days God is so faithful to send me gentle reminders that "this too shall pass"— and when it does I might even value these little mishaps.

One day I was somewhere between cleaning green throat spray mixed with little puddles of a potty accident on my white bedroom carpet and finding blue crayon stripes up the stairwell wall that I felt my motherhood joy slipping away. Even my attempts to read my youngest a fairy tale were thwarted when she told me I looked just like the lady in the book— only she didn't point to the princess but to the rather plump maid in the background. I became overwhelmed and very frustrated. I remembered praying for patience—but did God have to teach me enough for a lifetime all in one day? Even Calgon couldn't take me away.

Then several days later God sent one of those sweet reminders to keep life in perspective. We were visiting my husband's family when I discovered a hidden treasure inside a piece of furniture. I had admired the little olive-green letter desk on many previous visits but had never peeked inside. My mother-in-law and I were looking at it together when I opened the door covering the desk and there was my husband's name scratched into the paint in little boy script. That sealed the fate of the little green desk—I made sure Mom knew my desire to one day inherit this special piece of furniture. In the eyes of a professional antique collector the monetary value may be small but to me its flaw made the desk priceless.

Later that night as I lay in bed the thought struck me that what I consider a precious marking today was probably a cause of great frustration to his mother many years ago. Yet today, many years later, she treasures this little mishap. Isn't it funny how perspective changed an adverse situation into something that added great value and character to that green desk? The key word here is *perspective*. We must realize that motherhood is a high calling worth all the sleepless nights, endless messes, stains on the carpet, smudges on the walls, and dents in the car. Franklin D. Roosevelt said, "No other success in life—not being President, or being wealthy, or going to college, or writing a book, or anything else—comes up to the success of the man or woman who can feel that they have done their duty and that their children and grandchildren rise up and call them blessed."

The Toughest Job I've Ever Loved

I love to watch my children sleeping. I am so amazed by these wonderful gifts from heaven and I thank God for them. However, there have been times I've caught myself wishing for easier days when my children will be older. Wishing for more quiet times with less squealing; the opportunity to go to the potty without an audience; the freedom to go out to lunch with my friends at a restaurant that doesn't have a playground; and clean walls in my home minus the crayon, pen, and lipstick smears. But you know what? If I keep wishing away the present in hopes of an easier future, I am going to miss out on some of the most precious years of my children's lives. I want to always remember that feeling of desperation that I felt in the hospital for Ashley to just live. When we didn't know if Ashley was going to live or die, nothing would have made me happier than for her to squeal, follow me to the potty, interrupt my lunch, or color on the walls.

Yes, these days can be challenging, but let me encourage you to find God's gifts of joy and blessed rewards that await you every day as a mother. One day I'm going to clean smears from my walls for the last time, make our last playground trip, and realize the giggles and squeals have been silenced. It is my prayer that I haven't wished my time away, but rather that I discovered God's purpose for me as a mother and made the most of the toughest job I've ever loved.

The Writing on the Wall
There will come a day for finer things,
like sipping tea from a china cup
and time to read what the mailman brings.

For long peaceful bubble baths
and fine lace dresses,
perfectly shaped lipstick
and eating without messes.

And on that day I'll wish for even finer things,
like playing tea party with plastic cups
and little weed flowers that chubby hands bring.

For giggles and squeals
and hand-me-down dresses,
lipstick smeared faces
and other childhood blessings.

When the house is empty,
I'll hear echoes in the hall
and I'll long for interruptions
and writings on the wall.[1]

I wrote this poem one day when I was struggling over the daily tasks required of being a mother. I was longing for someone to remind me that the investment I am giving my children today really will make a difference in the future. The Lord gave me this poem to remind me that I am experiencing one of the finest times in life right now. I am helping shape and mold three beautiful daughters. I am taking part in creating eternally significant lives.

Being a mother is a gift from God. We don't ever need to wonder if what we do as mothers matters or not. It matters now, and it matters for eternity. The decisions we make in raising our children, the characters we help mold and shape, the little people who want to be just like us are the future leaders of the world. They are the ones who will pass on the values we hold dear to the generations to come. They will hold the awesome responsibility to go into all the world and share the good news of the gospel. They will be the living proof of the legacy we leave behind.

Developing a Loving Legacy

When I was a little girl I was terrified of the dark, and when that was combined with my very active imagination it produced all kinds of creepy-crawly monsters and villains. So I really should not have questioned my own daughters' fears of the dark. However my compassion started to wear thin after one too many nights in bed with Mommy and Daddy. Then I got smart and started leaving a light on at night that broke the fear.

Isn't it amazing how a little bit of light can make a world of difference? Psalm 119:105 (KJV) says, "Thy word is a lamp unto my feet, and light unto my path." Only God's Word can break the darkness we sometimes experience during our parental journey. When God commanded Joshua to "be strong and courageous" in Joshua 1:6–9, He also gave specific instructions for leading the Israelites into the Promised Land.

Mothers are leaders much like Joshua. We are to guide and instruct our children in the way of the Lord as the Bible instructs us to do. We, like Joshua, must be strong and courageous because we are leading God's little people. We must be careful to obey all the laws of the Lord, not turning from them to the right or the left, that we may be successful wherever we go. Meditate on God's Word day and night and be careful to do what is commanded; then you will be prosperous and successful. Again, be strong and courageous and do not be discouraged for God will be with you wherever you go.

Oh, what hope these Scriptures give me. As long as I let God's Word be my guide, I can rest assured knowing that I am building a legacy of love and fulfilling my purpose as a mother. In seeking to build my legacy, I had a divine revelation one day while reading Psalm 19:14, which says, "May the words of my mouth and the meditation of my heart be pleasing in your sight, O Lord, my Rock and my Redeemer." From this Scripture I wrote out what I call "The Pleasing Principles," an acrostic based on the word *pleasing*. These are the things that I want to do as a mother so that I can be pleasing to the Lord and create a loving legacy.

P—Positive Attitude

I think one of the greatest gifts a mother can give her children is the gift of a positive attitude. This is something that is more easily caught than taught. Children tend to mimic the attitudes they see exemplified within their homes by those who are closest to them. Having a positive attitude has nothing to do with the circumstances one faces, but rather how one chooses to react. Having the right attitude often means the difference between a full, happy life and a life dictated by the circumstances one faces.

L—Loving Spirit

The Bible tells us in 1 Corinthians 13 that we can do all kinds of great things, but if we do not have love it means nothing. The important thing to remember about love is that it is a decision, not a feeling. There are times when I don't feel that gushy-loving feeling toward one of my family members, but I choose to keep a loving spirit. The opposite of a loving spirit is a critical spirit. A critical spirit seeks to tear down, whereas a loving spirit seeks to fill in the gaps with a pure, Christlike love. A critical spirit seeks to fix problems out of annoyance and frustration. A loving spirit seeks God for wisdom to know when to step in and help and when to let go and let God.

E—Excited about their positive qualities

Children need encouragement. My mom was a great encourager. I've often told people that she was like a gold miner in my life. A gold miner goes into a mine looking for gold and doesn't mind having to sift through tons of dirt to get just a few small nuggets of gold. That's the way we should view our children's lives. We should be willing to move past the messy noses, bad attitudes, and other shortcomings of our kids in order to mine the nuggets of unique and wonderful qualities. Just as a miner gets excited about each nugget of gold discovered, we should get excited about each positive quality we uncover in our children and look for ways to encourage them.

A—Accepting despite their negative qualities

Acceptance is an absolute necessity for raising healthy, confident kids. If children feel loved and accepted at home, they won't go looking outside the home to have these needs met. Accepting our children does not mean that there won't be negative qualities that need to be dealt with. The key is to let them know we accept them while giving loving guidance to help them improve.

S—Submissive to my husband

This may seem like a strange part of a legacy formula, but it is a very important aspect. A child's sense of security is built on the foundation of a solid relationship between his mother and father. God designed marriage, and the way He has instructed it to work best is for the husband to submit to God and the wife to submit to the husband. This does not make the wife any less of a partner. If the husband loves and protects her as the Bible instructs, the wife naturally wants to meet her husband's need to be the leader of the family. When this works correctly, it models a healthy view of the respect and love that makes a family solid.

I—Interested in their interests

Very few moms enjoy skateboarding; music with a fast, unnatural beat; or many of the other strange things kids are interested in. However, it is important to be "tuned in" to whatever interests our children spend their time pursuing. A mom who is tuned in is not necessarily present at every event, as this would be especially embarrassing for teenagers. However, she does her research and is aware of whom her children are with and what kinds of things they are doing. Keeping the lines of communication open is vital to staying tuned into the lives of our children.

N—Nurturing

Some friends of mine, Randy and Patti McCoy, shared with me a beautiful way to nurture children. They wrote a blessing to say to their three boys. They use this as a way to assure their kids of the value they and God place on their lives. Kids long for this kind of nurturing and confidence building. I was so touched by their blessing I've included it in hopes that it would inspire you to write a similar blessing for your children:

> My son, you are a special boy,
> You bring us laughter, pride, and joy.
> God gave you as a gift to me.
> We need you in our family.
> And as you grow up brave and true,
> Remember that the Lord loves you.
> I pray for you the best of life;
> A happy home and a Christian wife.
> Teach your children about Jesus, too.
> And be the best at whatever you do.
> Remember this blessing as the days go by.
> Because God loves you, and so do I.
> —Randall R. McCoy[2]

Randy said, "The book *The Gift of the Blessing,* by John Trent and Gary Smalley, had a big impact on my life. This poem was my way of using the five elements of the traditional Hebrew blessing, presented in their book, to create a simple rhyme that my children could memorize and pass along (hopefully!) to their children. The effect it has had on my children has been wonderful. They can't wait to hear it. Plus, at major birthdays I give them a special blessing in which everyone present participates."

G—Growing as a godly woman

Abraham Lincoln said, "I regard no man as poor who has a godly mother." As I seek to pass on a legacy for my children, I know that no amount of wealth can ever compare to an inheritance of godly character modeled by their mother. I also know that I can't take my children any further down the road of spiritual maturity than what I've traveled. I must continue to grow and allow God to transform me into a godly woman worthy to be followed.

Your Purpose as a Mother

Family snuggle time is a tradition in the TerKeurst home. Many mornings our daughters sleepily make their way downstairs to crawl in bed with Mommy and Daddy to start their day with some good old-fashioned snuggling. There are plenty of good morning kisses and giggles to go around.

On one such morning, Hope, my oldest, decided to play the piggy game with her little sister's toes. We've played this game many times, but that day her rhyme caught me by surprise. "This little piggy goes to aerobics, and this little piggy goes to a meeting. This little piggy goes to the grocery store, and this little piggy goes to swim lessons." I was quite tickled by her rendition of the familiar rhyme; however, the thought struck me that none of her piggies stayed at home.

I decided it was time to rethink how we were spending our most precious commodity—time. Time to nurture and teach our children in the ways of the Lord. Time to sit and read. Time to play hide-and-go-seek, beauty shop, and cowboys and Indians. Time to share secrets. Time to kiss scraped knees and tear-stained faces. Time for imaginations and childhood dreams. Time for listening about first loves and comforting broken hearts. Time to cheer them on to victory in all of life's races.

Now don't get me wrong—I'm not saying that going to aerobics, the grocery store, and meetings are bad things—except when they crowd out time with our children. Life needs to be kept in balance, and then all things run more smoothly. Ecclesiastes 3:1 says, "There is a time for everything, and a season for every activity under heaven." Don't miss out on the precious time you have with your children today, because your children are only young for a season. I want to hear Hope's version go something like this: "This little piggy played hide-and-seek and this one read stories. This one ran errands and this one fixed dinner. But this one exclaimed "Yea!" as we all headed home."[3]

That's my purpose as a mother. It is my responsibility to make my home a place where my children look forward to coming back to, a place where they know they are safe, loved, and accepted. I must be available and tuned in to whatever they are facing in their lives. Praying for my children is the greatest way for me to guard and protect them, and teaching them biblical truths is the greatest wisdom I can share. Modeling the love of Christ is the best example I can set, and pursuing an on going relationship with the Lord is the most wonderful gift I can pass on.

WORKING ON YOUR JOURNAL

Take time to work on Section 2, Part 12, of your journal. If you have *The Life Planning Journal for Women,* turn there now. (The questions listed below are already included in the journal itself.) If you are making your own journal, transfer the questions below to your journal and spend some time recording your answers. Then remember to complete each step of the P.U.R.P.O.S.E. model described in chapter 9.

Once you complete this section of your journal, continue your reading with chapter 13, "There's No Place Like Home: Finding My Purpose as a Keeper of the Home."

QUESTIONS TO CONSIDER IN YOUR JOURNAL

1. Read Isaiah 49:16 and record it.

2. Do you trust God to hold on to your children? Journal your thoughts here.

3. Do you ever catch yourself losing your joy in this adventure known as motherhood?

4. Has God ever sent you an experience that helped you keep things in perspective as a mom? Journal that experience.

5. Have you ever caught yourself wishing away your children's childhood? Journal your thoughts after reading the poem "The Writing on the Wall."

6. List some ways you are helping shape the eternally significant lives of your children.

7. Read Joshua 1:6–9 and journal how God speaks to your heart through these verses.

8. Read over "The Pleasing Principles" and list some that you are doing well.

9. Now write down some principles you need to work on.

10. If you desire to write a blessing for your children, take time to work on it now. Once you complete it, write it out.

11. What is the greatest way for you to guard and protect your children?

12. What is the greatest wisdom you can share?

13. What is the best example you can set?

14. What is the greatest gift you can pass on?

Notes

1. The poem "The Writing on the Wall" and the section "The Toughest Job I've Ever Loved" are adapted from "The Writing on the Wall," *The Proverbs 31 Woman*, Sample Issue, by Lysa TerKeurst, and are used by permission of the author.

2. The poem by Randall R. McCoy is used by permission of the author.

3. The section "Your Purpose as a Mother" is adapted from "None of the Piggies Stayed Home," by Lysa TerKeurst, in *The Best of the Proverbs 31 Ministry: Encouragement and Inspiration for Women* (Charlotte, N.C.: The Proverbs 31 Ministry, 1999), 106–7, and is used by permission of the author.

Chapter Thirteen

THERE'S NO PLACE LIKE HOME: FINDING MY PURPOSE AS A KEEPER OF THE HOME

PRINCIPLE #4: The Proverbs 31 woman is a disciplined and industrious keeper of the home who creates a warm and loving environment for her family and friends.

In the last three chapters we prepared our hearts for some of our most important relationships. Now let's focus on the place those relationships are nurtured. It has been said that a home is a woman's self-portrait. I believe this to be true. You see, just as an artist paints not from his hands but his heart, so we women do the same. We may use our hands to tidy and clean, but the inspiration to turn a house into a home comes from within. It comes from the soft, tender spots of our hearts that long to tuck our family safely under our wings. We love to gather soft things and line our little nests so that they are comfortable and warm. Our homes are our places of love that we circle around those for whom we care so deeply.

In this chapter we'll talk about filling our homes with rare and beautiful treasures; take a peek at being organized, sanitized, and keeping our sanity; look at why we need to keep our arms strong for our tasks; and, finally, consider what our purpose is as keepers of our homes. Susannah Wesley, mother of John, the great theologian, and Charles, the amazing hymn writer, as well as many other children, said, "I am content to fill a little space if God be in it." May your heart be content and may your home be filled with laughter, love, and above all else, God.

Filling Your Home with Rare and Beautiful Treasures

When I was in elementary school we had a new student who came one day complete with a chauffeur and a bodyguard. I was amazed by this girl and felt sorry for the attention that surrounded her that first day. Soon she was like any other student, and one day on the playground we became friends. I learned later that she was the governor's daughter, which didn't mean much to me until the first time she invited me over to play at her house. I was amazed by the stately rooms and beautifully groomed gardens. Our favorite room to play in, however, was not stately or beautifully decorated. It was a small closet where my friend kept her dolls. We spent hours changing diapers, naming babies, and pretending to be moms. These are wonderful childhood memories. They prove to me that children are not impressed by the trappings of the adult world. I remember thinking that my friend's house was pretty, but that there was no place I'd rather be in that whole mansion than the little closet.

Children are not enamored with lavishly decorated homes. They simply want a safe, fun environment where they can play, learn, and grow up. They would rather have time with their mom and dad than all the material possessions in the world. The best thing to fill your home with is love. Proverbs 24:3 says, "By wisdom a house is built, and through understanding it is established; through knowledge its rooms are filled with rare and beautiful treasures."

A loving family is a priceless treasure that is much more valuable than any material possession. Now don't get me wrong, I like to decorate and make my home a place that reflects my personality and feels homey. However, if you were to ask my children what their favorite things about our home were they would not list the window treatments, furniture, or wallpaper. They would say it's the fun times we spend together. These are the times we develop our children's character, get to know what makes them tick, and nurture parent-child relationships that are open, honest, and fun. Here are some of the beautiful treasures I try and fill my home with:

Family Nights

We designate one night a week as family night in our home. We make it a fun time that everybody participates in. Sometimes we pop popcorn, rent kid's movies, and snuggle up together. Other times we go out to ethnic restaurants and teach our kids about traditions in other cultures. One of my favorites was when my kids decided they wanted to help some flood victims, so we put together a booth to sell calendars and then donated the proceeds to a local charity. It's not what we do that matters as much as letting our children know that they can count on spending some special time set aside just for them.

Date Nights with Daddy

These are some of my daughters' most favorite nights out. About once a month, my husband takes his little girls on a special date. Sometimes it's one-on-one and other times they all get to go as a group. This gives them a proper view of how they are to be treated on a date and gives Daddy some special time to build up his daughters' self-esteem.

Books and Games

Because television watching is limited in our home, the kids have found creative ways to entertain themselves. Games are a favorite activity for my older two daughters. Many times my husband and I join in the fun, which gives us great opportunities to teach lessons on playing fair and being good sports. We also make it a point to read to our children before they go to bed. Bible story books, a children's Bible, books that teach virtue, and John Trent's book *Bedtime Blessings* (Focus on the Family) are some of our favorites.

Kids' Artwork

I can remember the happiness I felt when my mom would hang up my artwork in our home. She still has some of my artistic creations around the home all these many years later. She was careful to never criticize my work, but always let me know that she was proud of my talents. I now do this for my own kids. This teaches my children that I value their efforts and am proud of their accomplishments.

Family Traditions

One thing I feel that is vital for my children to have is a sense of real belonging. One of the best ways to build this security in the heart of a child is to establish special traditions unique to your family. For example, we have a tradition of a unique way to say I love you. Instead of the normal "I love you, I love you, too" dialogue exchange, we say, "I love you more than chocolate cake," or "I love you more than purple pansies," or any one of the other things our kids know that we really like. They reply back, "I love you more than my Elizabeth doll . . . more than powder-sugar doughnuts . . . more than the world." The objects change almost every time, but the message is clear—there is nothing in the world that any of us love more than each other.

You Are Special

Take time to celebrate your family members' special achievements. We have a special red plate that is used for those "way to go" days. As I mentioned earlier, I record these events in a red "Success Journal" that will be enjoyed for years to come. This is a great way to let your child, spouse, or even a dinner guest know how truly special he or she is. We also make a point of reminding our kids that they are special on those not-so-good days. You know—the ones where someone has made fun of them, they made a bad grade, or one of the other hundreds of ways tender hearts get broken. Looking through the Success Journal is a good way to get cheered up. Sometimes we pull out Max Lucado's book *You Are Special* and remind our daughters that no matter what others might say, God says they are special. Other times we might go out for ice cream and just talk. The most important thing is that our kids know that we are on their side, willing to be there for them as they fight their battles.

Scrapbooks

My kids' favorite books to look at and read are the scrapbooks I've made for them. I put all of our pictures in these books and journal about the fun times we've shared. I also write letters to my children so that they will have their mother's love recorded in a permanent place. "You may have tangible wealth untold, caskets of jewels and coffers of gold. Richer than I you can never be; I have a mother who made a scrapbook for me!"[1]

After-School Snack Time

Every child desires two things: love and acceptance. If we can make our homes places where they find these, then home is where they'll want to be. If our kids feel safe to talk to us, then hopefully we will be the ones they will choose to confide in. One way I have made sure my kids know that their mommy cares about their concerns and wants to share in their joys is to have a daily snack time. This is where I call time-out from everyone's activities and fix a yummy snack—and we sit down at the kitchen table together. We talk about our day, tell funny jokes, review papers sent home from school, and share whatever else might be on their hearts.

You probably have some of the same kinds of treasures in your home. Always remember that these things are rare, beautiful, and worth protecting. I have to make a conscious effort to make sure the busyness of life does not crowd out these precious things from my family's life. I do it because I know that after all is said and done and I look back on this time of building my legacy, the little things really will have mattered.

Organized, Sanitized, and Keeping Your Sanity

When I went off to college, I thought I was very prepared. I had new books, new pencils, new clothes, and a meal ticket to the dining hall. I adored my new roommate and loved the way we decorated our dorm room. Everything went really well for the first couple of months until our closet became so overloaded with my dirty clothes that my sweet roommate decided to confront me. Keeping my clothes clean was not a chore I was responsible for at home, so I had no clue how to do it once I was away from home. I guess I kept waiting for the laundry fairy to swoop into my dorm, sprinkle some magic dust over my clothes, wave her wand—and my clothes would all be clean, folded, and put back into my drawers.

My roommate assured me she was no laundry fairy, but for the sake of her sanity she would teach me the basics of operating a washing machine. The first lesson for Laundry 101 was the art of separation. She instructed me to separate the clothes into three piles while she went down to the Laundromat to reserve all available machines. When she returned she instantly knew she was dealing with a cleaning-challenged individual. I had separated my clothes with pants and skirts in one pile, shirts in another, and everything else in pile number three. The whole colors versus whites thing never even entered my mind.

Well, needless to say, I've come a long way since that first lesson and have now done enough laundry to have earned a master's degree in the field, if there is such a thing. I have also learned that sheets should be washed more than once a year and that toilets can be cleaned before fuzzy things grow in them. You would be quite impressed by my vacuuming and dusting abilities and by the fact that I now know why they sell specifically designed powders to use in the dishwasher instead of liquid dish soap. (Just use your imagination on how I learned that lesson the hard way.) There is one area, however, that I've had to continually work at—organization.

One winter I had a major attitude adjustment that really helped me improve my organizational skills. It all started when my husband and I were getting ready to go on a vacation. Art asked me if I knew where our ski gear was located. I had no idea. I felt like saying, "Look,

I am a servant of our Lord and Savior Jesus Christ; I am responsible for three very active children; I keep up with laundry, soap scum, menus, social schedules, pest control, and doctor and dentist appointments. So what if I can't find the ski gear!" Then Proverbs 31:27 started to creep in and adjust my attitude: "She watches over the affairs of her household." Then another thought really knocked me for a loop. If Jesus Christ, the Savior of the world, God's Son, could come and labor in a carpenter's shop, how dare I cop an attitude about watching over the affairs of my household? Well, we left for vacation having found most of what we needed for our trip and nine long hours of driving time for my husband to encourage me to take on a new attitude toward keeping our home in order.

Now, if you were to ask my friends who frequently popped over to see me in those early days, they would have told you that my house appeared pretty tidy. But there were some trouble areas that really needed some attention. So I tackled the first of those projects when we returned from vacation—my closet. Ecclesiastes 3:6 tells us that "there is a time to keep and a time to throw away." So I walked into my closet with a new passion for order and walked out with ten garbage bags full of give-away, throw-away, and put-elsewhere items. It was so freeing! (I know you naturally superneat people reading this are probably in shock that someone could fill ten garbage bags with things that should never have been in a bedroom closet. Please realize that God made people like me to add a little creativity to the world of homemaking.)

Terry Willits, in her book *Creating a Sensational Home,* says, "Beauty replenishes while disorder drains. Disorder causes confusion and clutters the mind; it distracts your eyes from enjoying that which is beautiful."[2] It was amazing that when I took out the clothes I never wore and made room for my favorites to hang in an orderly fashion, I felt like I had more to wear than ever! I am happy to say that I have since tackled several other trouble spots in my home and I am that much closer to being able to say, "I am organized!" The more organized my home becomes, the more beautiful it feels and I enjoy being at home more! The most important thing about this whole process has been my attitude. I believe that with a good and joyful attitude even the most overwhelming jobs can get done and might even be fun. Remember, "Well done is better than well said" (Ben Franklin).

Here are some ideas to get you started:

- As a part of the "Goals" you list for this section of your journal, make a list of projects that need to be tackled.
- Divide larger projects into smaller action steps that can be accomplished on their assigned day.
- Schedule time each week to tackle a project.
- Play some upbeat praise music while you work.
- Have a designated place in mind to take those give-away items. (These items may also be good for a garage sale. If so, set a date for your sale and work to get all your trouble areas organized before that date. Then after your sale, take all that is left over to a charity—don't save it for another garage sale!)
- Reward yourself for a job well done with a bubble bath after the kids go to bed.
- Develop a plan to keep the areas you've worked on organized.

Keeping Your Arms Strong for the Tasks

A lot of energy is required to do all that women do. This was true over two thousand years ago when the Proverbs 31 woman was busy going about her work vigorously, and it still holds true today. It's exhausting wiping bottoms and noses, dusting dressers, and rinsing dishes—and then single-handedly rescuing the baby from the stairs and the four-year-old from the creepy crawly spider that's got her screaming in the living room, fixing a broken necklace for my six-year-old, and all the while carrying on a conversation with my friend, who is doing the same on the other end of the line. I must be faster than an overflowing toilet, stronger than the will of my toddler, and able to leap tall loads of laundry in a single bound. The thought of purposely expending energy after doing all of this just doesn't seem reasonable or sane for a keeper of the home, does it? Well, there was a reason the Proverbs 31 woman knew to keep her arms strong for her tasks (Proverbs 31:17), so read on.

Does the very word *exercise* conjure up feelings of guilt and dread? Well, it certainly used to for me. I can tell you with all honesty that I used to cry at the thought of working out. Now, amazingly, I actually enjoy both exercising and the benefits I get from it. I realized that exercising was the best way for me to keep my energy level up, my emotions leveled out, and my weight down. So how did I move past the guilt and dread and into an exercise program?

First of all, it took a lot of prayer. I prayed daily for the Lord's help. I prayed that He would help me fit exercise into my schedule. I prayed that He would give me the energy to get started. I memorized Philippians 4:13, which says, "I can do everything through him who gives me strength," and recited it often. I also prayed for God to send me people to encourage me and friends to work out with me. God was so faithful and answered all my prayers.

The second attitude changer in my life was my very encouraging husband. He has always been active and has the energy and positive attitude to show for it. I read in a fitness magazine that depression and fatigue are often the result of not getting enough exercise. Art encouraged me to develop a realistic workout plan and then stick to it. He helped me set up short- and long-term goals, which I wrote down to track my progress. Art became my accountability partner and learned what did and did not motivate me. Since I am very motivated by prizes, we wrote into my plan the rewards I would get with each goal met.

Lastly, I got educated. I have always had a fear of the unknown, and because I did not know a lot about the human body and the benefits of exercise, I always feared getting started. However, when I got educated on the facts, knowledge itself became a motivator. Here's a simple version of what I learned:

- One pound of fat equals 3,500 calories.
- It is a safe and realistic goal to lose one pound per week until I get to my goal weight.
- I can exercise off 350 calories per day multiplied by four workout days, which equals 1,400 burned calories.

- I can cut my daily caloric intake by 300 calories, which over a week equals a 2,100 calorie reduction in intake.
- 1,400 burned calories plus a 2,100 reduced weekly caloric intake equals 3,500 calories, or one pound lost per week.

It is important to consult with a physician before starting any type of diet and exercise program in order to learn what is safe, effective, and realistic for you. I went to a local YMCA facility and consulted with a fitness pro, who helped me figure out my aerobic heart rate training zone and how long I needed to do certain aerobic activities to burn the necessary number of calories. Because I have small children, I invested in a stair master to use in my home. I also enjoy running when the weather is nice and my husband is home to watch the kids. Each person is different and will have to develop a plan for the most realistic way to find time to exercise and which type of exercise she enjoys doing. Let me encourage you to start today on the road to a healthier, happier, stronger, and more vigorous you.

Your Purpose as the Keeper of Your Home

One of my favorite movies of all time is *The Wizard of Oz*. In the movie, Dorothy dreams of getting out of Kansas, and soon—thanks to a most unusual tornado—finds herself in the colorful world of Oz. The rest of the movie tells of her journey down a yellow brick road that she hopes will lead her home. When she finally gets to the wizard, he instructs her to repeat five words over and over: "There's no place like home, there's no place like home, there's no place like home ..." That's our purpose as keepers of the home: to create a safe haven for our families where they know they will find a loving wife and mother who seeks with all her heart to create a nurturing environment.

I must always remember the incredible opportunities God has given me as a keeper of a home. I must remember to keep an attitude of thanksgiving as I wash the clothes, clean the kitchen, make the beds, and pick up the toys. What a privilege it is to have a place to call home and people who look to me to make it lovely. Each night as I tuck my girls into bed I try to remember to lift up a prayer of thanksgiv-

ing for the opportunity I have to hear three little ones call me Mommy. Then as I go to bed and feel the arms of my husband wrap around me, I need to thank God again for the honor of being someone's wife. It's an awesome purpose but one that reaps incredible rewards. As our families head out into this crazy world, their hearts are anchored to a safe place, and they, like Dorothy, know that there truly is no place like home.

WORKING ON YOUR JOURNAL

Take time to work on Section 2, Part 13, of your journal. If you have *The Life Planning Journal for Women,* turn there now. (The questions listed below are already included in the journal itself.) If you are making your own journal, transfer the questions below to your journal and spend some time recording your answers. Then remember to complete each step of the P.U.R.P.O.S.E. model described in chapter 9.

Once you complete this section of your journal, continue your reading with chapter 14, "Time and Money: Finding My Purpose as a Faithful Steward."

QUESTIONS TO CONSIDER IN YOUR JOURNAL

1. Is it evident that God's love fills your home?
2. Read Proverbs 24:3 and record it. Why or why not?
3. Besides material possessions, what rare and beautiful treasures fill your home?
4. What would your family say are their favorite parts of your home?
5. Read Proverbs 31:27. How do you watch over the affairs of your household?
6. Do you have a plan for keeping your home clean and in order?

7. Ask each member of your family what his or her definition of a "haven" is. Record their responses.

8. How do you keep your arms strong for your tasks?

9. What are some creative ways you could fit exercising into your schedule?

10. Do you consider it a privilege to be the keeper of your home?

11. Journal what you are most thankful for.

Notes

1. Adapted from *The Reading Mother*, by Strickland Gillian. Retold from the *Creative Memories Design and Layout Ideas Book*, 3:67.

2. Terry Willits, *Creating a Sensational Home: Awakening the Senses to Bring Life and Love to Your Home* (Grand Rapids: Zondervan, 1996).

Chapter Fourteen

TIME AND MONEY: FINDING MY PURPOSE AS A FAITHFUL STEWARD

PRINCIPLE #5: The Proverbs 31 woman contributes to the financial well-being of her household by being a faithful steward of the time and money God has entrusted to her.

In the last several chapters, we have looked at some of our most special relationships and the place we nurture them. Now let's examine God's amazing provision for His children and our responsibility to manage all that He entrusts to us. In this chapter we'll discover why we should not bite off more than we can chew, should seek to understand time well spent, learn basic principles for managing our money, and finally arrive at our purpose as a faithful steward. Throughout all we'll discuss during this chapter, I pray that one nugget of wisdom stays planted firmly in your heart: We must hold on tightly to God and loosely to the treasures of this world.

Alice Gray, in her book *More Stories for the Heart,* wrote a story, "The Treasure," about a little girl named Jenny that exemplifies this point beautifully.

The cheerful girl with bouncy golden curls was almost five. Waiting with her mother at the checkout stand, she saw them: a circle of glistening white pearls in a pink foil box.

"Oh please, Mommy. Can I have them? Please, Mommy, please!"

Quickly the mother checked the back of the little foil box and then looked back into the pleading blue eyes of her little girl's upturned face.

"A dollar ninety-five. That's almost $2. If you really want them, I'll think of some extra chores for you and in no time you can save enough money to buy them for yourself. Your birthday's only a week away and you might get another crisp dollar bill from Grandma."

As soon as Jenny got home, she emptied her piggy bank and counted out 17 pennies. After dinner, she did more than her share of chores and she went to the neighbor and asked Mrs. McJames if she could pick dandelions for ten cents. On her birthday, Grandma did give her another new dollar bill, and at last she had enough money to buy the necklace.

Jenny loved her pearls. They made her feel dressed up and grown up. She wore them everywhere—Sunday school, kindergarten, even to bed. The only time she took them off was when she went swimming or had a bubble bath. Mother said if they got wet, they might turn her neck green.

Jenny had a very loving daddy, and every night when she was ready for bed, he would stop whatever he was doing and come upstairs to read her a story. One night when he finished the story, he asked Jenny, "Do you love me?"

"Oh, yes, Daddy. You know that I love you."

"Then give me your pearls."

"Oh, Daddy, not my pearls. But you can have Princess—the white horse from my collection. The one with the pink tail. Remember Daddy? The one you gave me. She's my favorite."

"That's OK, Honey, Daddy loves you. Good night." And he brushed her cheek with a kiss.

About a week later, after the story time, Jenny's daddy asked again, "Do you love me?"

"Daddy, you know I love you."

"Then give me your pearls."

"Oh, Daddy, not my pearls. But you can have my baby doll. The brand new one I got for my birthday. She is so beautiful and you can have the yellow blanket that matches her sleeper."

"That's OK. Sleep well. God bless you, little one. Daddy loves you." And as always, he brushed her cheek with a gentle kiss.

A few nights later when her daddy came in, Jenny was sitting on her bed with her legs crossed Indian-style. As he came close, he noticed her chin was trembling and one silent tear rolled down her cheek.

"What is it, Jenny? What's the matter?"

Jenny didn't say anything but lifted her little hand up to her daddy. And when she opened it, there was her little pearl necklace. With a little quiver, she finally said, "Here Daddy. It's for you."

With tears gathering in his own eyes, Jenny's kind daddy reached out with one hand to take the dime-store necklace, and with the other hand he reached into his pocket and pulled out a blue velvet case with a strand of genuine pearls and gave them to Jenny. He had had them all the time. He was just waiting for her to give up the dime-store stuff so he could give her genuine treasure.

So like our heavenly Father.[1]

Biting Off More Than You Can Chew

Mealtimes have been an adventure since I've had children. I remember my romantic notions of motherhood before children and I can't help laughing at my naïveté. Our dinner table would be adorned with fresh flowers and cloth napkins. Little ones with rosy faces and pristine dresses would eagerly await the gourmet meal set before them. Well, very rarely do flowers adorn our table because inevitably one of the children would eat them instead of dinner. We use paper napkins, paper towels, and Wipies—not cloth napkins. The faces are messy instead of rosy and the dresses are stained. As far as the gourmet meals, the children prefer Chef Boyardee and most times they have to be bribed to eat that. It was during one such bribery session that I learned an important life lesson: Biting off more than you can chew can be hard on you and even more irritating to those around you.

You see, we have a rule in the TerKeurst home that you can't have dessert until you've eaten enough of your dinner. One night my daughter Hope decided to be smart and stuff a large portion of food in her mouth to hurry the process along. The only problem was that her mouth was too small and her gag reflex too strong. She proceeded to spit the contents of her overstuffed mouth into my hands.

I knew at that point that it would be many years before my dreams of cloth napkins and pristine dresses would come true. I also knew that there must be a life lesson in this mess—and there was. As I later reflected on this incident the thought occurred to me that many adults bite off more than they can chew and have to use someone else's hands to help them as well. Everything is so rushed today. Schedules are crammed full. Finances are stretched to their limit. People's tensions run high. And all for what? I think it's a shame to rush to the desserts of life only to find that nutrition and real satisfaction comes from the dinner. Let me encourage you to slow down, unpack your schedule, and reevaluate your finances. Dessert will be served in due time.

Here are some ideas to get you started:

- *Have a planning session with your spouse to discuss how well your family is managing the money God has entrusted to you.* Are you giving God your first fruits (Proverbs 3:9)? Are you saving and planning for your future? Are you living within your means? Remember the old saying: "If your outcome exceeds your income then your upkeep will be your downfall!"

- *Write out a realistic household budget.* If this is a new concept for you, I would encourage you to contact Christian Financial Concepts at P.O. Box 2377, Gainesville, Georgia 30503-2377, for information on getting started.

- *Evaluate your family's schedule.* Are you able to eat at least one meal a day together around your table? Let me encourage you to make this a priority for your family. Encourage discussions by asking questions such as: "If you could go back and change the way you did one thing today what would it be?" or, "If you could invite any three people to join us for dinner who would they be?"

- *Meet with your family once a week to discuss and plan that week's schedule.* We do this every Sunday afternoon. We make sure that everyone has input as to what night we will have our special family night and what we'll be doing. Also, my husband and I establish our date night for that week. This planning time also gives the kids a chance to let us know about any special events that Mom and Dad need to be aware of.

Time Well Spent

Most people judge an individual's wealth by what kind of house the person lives in, the car she drives, the clothes she wears, and the vacations she takes. I beg to differ. I think these things may show how much money a person has but not how wealthy she is. To me, wealth is defined by four simple letters: *TIME.* You see, money is something that can be earned, borrowed, and even stolen. Time, on the other hand, cannot. The wonderful thing about time is that we are all given the same amount each day to spend as we choose. The sad fact is that many of us don't spend our time doing the things that really matter in light of eternity.

A wealthy man is one who realizes what a precious gift time is and spends lavishly on God, his family, and ministering to those whom God sends his way. These are the things that will really matter when our time here on earth has all been spent and it is revealed where we are to spend our eternity. The Bible makes it very clear that only those who accept Jesus Christ as their Savior will spend eternity in heaven. I can't think of anything more important than spending time developing a relationship with God, who gives us this wonderful gift, and allowing Him to dictate how the rest of our time is spent.

Let me encourage you today to be in the business of spending time doing things of eternal value. As a wife and mother this helps me turn the most mundane tasks into eternally significant blessings. As I teach my children how to wash the dishes, I have time to tell about Jesus washing the disciples' feet. As I fold the mounds of laundry that greet me in the laundry room each day, I have time to pray for my husband, as he is at work so I can be at home. As I make a meal for a friend, I think of ways to meet other's physical needs so I might one day be able to share Jesus with them and help meet spiritual needs as well. No, I may not be wealthy by the world's definition, but having time to spend doing these things is better than any amount of money could ever be.

Managing Your Money

When Art and I first started dating he made a joke one day when he asked about my dowry. I had something I was bringing into our possible marriage and it started with the letter *D,* but it wasn't a dowry. It was debt. I assured him that my credit card debt was no big deal because I just paid the small required amount each month and I'd get around to paying the balance later. When we got engaged he informed me that the "later" had arrived and he wanted me to be debt free before we got married. I reluctantly agreed and started the long, hard process of getting out of debt. I cut up my credit cards, slashed my spending, and paid off my debts before our wedding day. After we got married, I continued to struggle. The problem wasn't that I didn't want to manage money well; it was that I honestly did not know how. Art took pride in balancing his checkbook to the penny—and remember, as I mentioned earlier, I thought as long as I had checks in my checkbook I must have money in my account. It took many financial heart-to-heart discussions to come to an understanding about a money management system that would work for our family. Art had to relax a little and I had to tighten the reins on my runaway spending, but eventually we came up with the B.E.S.T. plan for us.

B—Budget Wisely

You can use all kinds of fancy formulas and computer software to help you manage your money, but if you don't have a budget, things will eventually get out of balance. It's pretty simple: You can't spend more than you make, and the best way to keep this from happening is to establish a realistic budget and stick to it. Every year Art and I reevaluate our budget and talk about short-term and long-term financial goals. His goals usually center around investments and long-term security and mine around furniture and window treatments. We've come to realize that both are important and worth saving toward.

Our budget is pretty simple and can be broken down into four major categories:

- *Spending* (our mortgage, groceries, gas, clothing, medical bills, etc.)
- *Giving* (the tithe to our church, gifts to ministries, helping others in need)
- *Short-Term Saving* (vacations, Christmas, home improvement projects, furniture)
- *Long-Term Saving* (investments, retirement savings, college planning for our children)

Within each category we list each expenditure and determine a realistic amount that should be spent. After each expenditure has been listed, we carefully consider what our income will be for that year and balance our outflow with our inflow. While we may have to go through and cut certain expenditures to make the budget balance, we never cut from our giving category, as we are committed to giving back to God. We truly believe that setting a budget is the best way to manage our money and have seen tremendous financial benefits from this type of proactive approach to money management.

E—Examine Your Heart

When I was single, as I told you before, I was not very careful with my finances. Instead of managing my money, I felt in many ways controlled by it. I bought into the world's lie that you are defined by what you own, what kind of car you drive, and how you dress. For me, it was more than just poor banking skills that got me into trouble; it was a heart issue. I had voids in my life that I was trying to fill with illusive material possessions. I thought if I could just get one more nice outfit, or a nicer car, or live in a larger home then I would finally find the happiness and peace I was searching for. However, more was never enough because there was always something else better, another level to reach toward, another possession that I wanted. In seeking peace of mind this way, I got the exact opposite of what I desired. Instead of happiness and peace, I found I was living under a dark cloud of debt and discontentment.

God tells us in Hebrews 13:5, "Keep your lives free from the love of money and be content with what you have, because God has said, 'Never will I leave you; never will I forsake you.'" We must examine our hearts and seek to keep ourselves free from loving the fleeting things of this world. We must always hold our possessions with open hands, realizing they might be lost in an instant. However, we can find peace in the fact that God will never leave us, He knows our needs and has promised to care for us. You see, it's not wrong to enjoy nice things, but it is wrong to put our pursuit of material possessions ahead of our pursuit of God.

S—Stewardship Is Key

When I finally came to the realization that my money was not mine at all, my whole attitude toward money management changed. I learned that everything belongs to the Lord and that I am merely a steward of what He chooses to entrust to me. A good steward manages what has been entrusted to him as faithfully as the owner would. In other words, I am accountable to manage my finances as if God were the one writing the check, paying the bills, filing my taxes, and deciding how much to give, save, and spend. I must consult God through praying about purchases before they are made, not when I've overextended myself and am looking to have Him get me out of a crisis.

I believe that God wants to bring us to a place where we are content both in times of plenty and in times of need. I also believe that He wants us to hold our possessions with open hands, always willing to let go of anything God sees as a threat to a happy and content heart. Too many of us are holding onto the fleeting things of this world so tightly that we miss the genuine, lasting things God wants to give us. A faithful steward knows how to let go of worldly things in order to be able to accept God's best.

T—Teamwork Leads to Togetherness

Early on in our marriage, Art and I were in a Sunday school class for newly married couples. One Sunday our class was discussing whether or not married people should have separate bank accounts. One well-meaning couple made such a strong statement against this that I felt like melting into my chair. When it was our turn in the circle to tell how we managed our household account, my brave husband with great wisdom and confidence shared how we too believed in sharing our finances jointly. However, it was best for our family to have two joint accounts—one that was managed by him and the other his wife. This is what works most effectively for us.

We know that the answer to successfully working together to manage our finances isn't found in whether or not we share one bank account. It's working together as a team that leads to togetherness. It is Art's understanding that things like fabric and wallpaper are investments that are as important as stocks and bonds. It's me trusting Art when he says we need to wait to purchase things until we can pay for them in cash. It's Art trusting that his wife will manage her part of the budget well and look for ways to be thrifty. It's me not pressuring my husband by making him feel like we don't have enough. It's also me remembering to thank him for the way he provides for our family. Teamwork is a must for couples who want to avoid financial conflict in marriage. We have found that we must communicate our expectations and evaluate our budget at least once a month together. While it's not always easy to find the time, we know it makes a lot of "cents" to do so.

Your Purpose as a Faithful Steward

I woke up the other Saturday morning to the most beautiful sound. My three girls were upstairs laughing as they shared little girl secrets, tickled each other, and enjoyed all being together in Hope's bed. They were unaffected at that time of the morning by schedules, homework, and chores. They were spontaneously enjoying life, enjoying being together.

I wondered when in the process of changing from a child into an adult is the point where many of us lose our laughter and excitement about life. When was it that some of us stopped being amazed by sun-rises and sunsets, rainbows, blooming flowers, butterflies, and the many other miracles of God that surround us each day? Most of us would have loved to have been present when God parted the Red Sea, made the walls of Jericho fall just from the shouts of His people, and rolled the stone away as He raised His Son from the dead. Would those miracles have astounded us, or would we have lost them in the midst of busy schedules and over-stretched budgets?

Life itself is mysterious, miraculous, and filled with beauty. In find-ing our purpose as faithful stewards, we must remember who has en-trusted us with the time and resources we have been given. We must remember to take time to praise our Master for the miracles that sur-round us each day and to trust Him to provide for us just as He does for every part of His creation. Schedules, budgets, investments, and pay-ing the bills are all part of life, but they should never replace our de-pendence on God. Replace the worry you feel about your finances with responsible planning and a dependence on God.

Matthew 6:31–34 (LB) says,

So don't worry at all about having enough food and clothing. Why be like the heathen? For they take pride in all these things and are deeply concerned about them. But your heavenly Father already knows perfectly well that you need them, and will give them to you if you give him first place in your life and live as he wants you to. So don't be anxious about tomorrow. God will take care of your tomorrow too. Live one day at a time.

Regarding this Scripture, *The Life Application Bible* commentary says,

Planning for tomorrow is time well spent; worrying about tomorrow is time wasted. Sometimes it's difficult to tell the difference. Careful planning is thinking ahead about goals, steps, and schedules, and trust-ing in God's guidance. When done well it can alleviate worry. The worrier is consumed by fear and finds it difficult to trust God. The worrier lets his plans interfere with his relationship with God. Don't let worries about tomorrow affect your relationship with God today.[2]

Be a good manager of the time and money God has entrusted to you. God's miracles are all around you, reminding you that He will take care of you and that He is in control. I pray that you will rediscover the lost art of waking up with giggles and smiles, unaffected by the pressures of life and full of the blessed assurance of a child whose Father knows well her needs and who will provide.

WORKING ON YOUR JOURNAL

Take time to work on Section 2, Part 14, of your journal. If you have *The Life Planning Journal for Women,* turn there now. (The questions listed below are already included in the journal itself.) If you are making your own journal, transfer the questions below to your journal and spend some time recording your answers. Then remember to complete each step of the P.U.R.P.O.S.E. model described in chapter 9.

Once you complete this section of your journal, continue your reading with chapter 15, "The Gift of Godly Friendships: Finding My Purpose as a Godly Friend."

QUESTIONS TO CONSIDER IN YOUR JOURNAL

1. What "dime-store" stuff are you holding onto?
2. What genuine treasure might God have for you?
3. Are you giving God your firstfruits (Proverbs 3:9)?
4. Are you saving and planning for your future? If yes, how? If not, why not?
5. Are you living within your means?
6. Are you able to eat at least one meal with your family gathered together at your table?
7. How would you define wealthy?
8. How valuable is time to you?

9. Do you spend your time and money investing in things of eternal value?

10. Do you have a budget? If yes, what benefits have you seen from having a budget? If no, how might a budget help you manage your money better?

11. Read Hebrews 13:5 and journal your thoughts about this verse.

12. Are you putting your pursuit of material things ahead of your pursuit of God? Journal your thoughts.

13. Write a description of a faithful steward.

14. Are you and your husband working together as a team in the area of finances?

15. Read Matthew 6: 31–34. Journal your thoughts.

Notes

1. Excerpted from *More Stories for the Heart,* © 1997. Compiled by Alice Gray. Used by permission of Multnomah Publishers, Inc.

2. *Life Application Bible: The Living Bible* (Wheaton, Ill.: Tyndale, 1988), notes on Matthew 6:31–34, p. 1338.

Chapter Fifteen

THE GIFT OF GODLY FRIENDSHIPS: FINDING MY PURPOSE AS A GODLY FRIEND

PRINCIPLE #6: The Proverbs 31 woman speaks with wisdom and faithful instruction as she mentors and supports other women and develops godly friendships.

One day one of my little girls shrieked with excitement as she ran into the house with a new special friend. Only this "friend" did not have pigtails and bright rosy cheeks; it had a small, tubelike, furry body with green stripes and black dots. The fact that their physical appearances were not similar did not seem to matter at all. She loved her friend. As a matter of fact, she loved her friend a little too much, and we attended his funeral that same afternoon.

Strangely enough, I learned some valuable lessons about friendships that day. I learned that it's not a good idea to hold our friends too loosely or too tightly. Too loosely and they'll crawl away. Too tightly and they'll feel smothered. It's not a good idea to pick things off of our friends that we might not like. We need to love them how they are and prayerfully leave the rest with God. It's not a good idea to let our friends crawl all over us, as we'll inevitably get pooped on. Friends that are always putting us down and condemning us are not really friends.

I also learned some things that are good ideas. It is a good idea to love others no matter how different they are. The color of our skin is not as important as what is in our hearts. It is a good idea to pick a friend up and spend some time playing together. Laughing and having fun rejuvenate the soul. It is a good idea to look at our friends as caterpillars sometimes. Though they may get wrapped up in their own cocoons at times, if we wait patiently, love unconditionally, and cheer them on, we may get to witness God's miracle of one rising to new heights. Let me invite you to join me now as we look at the beautiful blessing of friendship. We'll examine the friendship circles, why it's important to invest ourselves in the lives of others, the ABC's of taming the tongue, and our purpose as a godly friend.

The Friendship Circles

When I was little, my best friend's name was Rabbit. I loved this friend of mine. She had soft pink fur, a head that tilted from side to side if the music box inside her was wound, and she fit perfectly in the crook of my neck when I slept. She made me feel secure and safe. She loved to listen to my secrets and she never betrayed my confidence. Her ears wiped many a tear from my eyes and her discolored and worn body showed evidence of something that was well loved. If only my adult friendships could be so easy and comfortable.

However, Rabbit had a flaw that caused our friendship to go by the wayside as I grew older. Once I realized that Rabbit could only talk in my imagination, it grew increasingly difficult to communicate with her. I needed to hear another person's ideas, advice, and encouragement. So what was once easy and comfortable was traded for riskier people-relationships. Just like all of us, I needed the human touch of a friend.

Over the years I have been blessed with wonderful, caring friends. I know I can't make it without other women's love, support, advice, and fellowship. I also know that because my friends have such an incredible influence on my life, I must choose them carefully and wisely. The best friendship model I know to follow is that of Jesus. Isn't it amazing that even He needed friends? He needed their companionship, support, love, and fellowship just as you and I do. Jesus was wise in choosing His friends and in knowing how many it was realistic to have. Examine Jesus' model as outlined in the chart "The Friendship Circles" and give some thought to the relationships in your life.

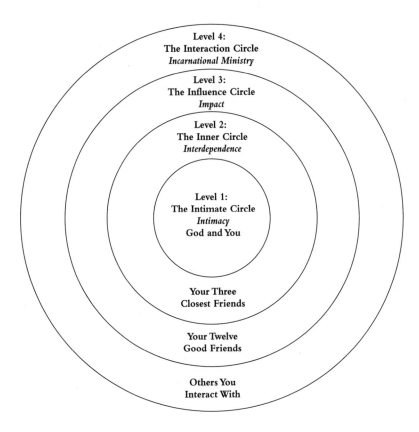

Level 1: The Intimate Circle

The word that characterizes this first circle is *intimacy*. In Jesus' life we see this portrayed in Matthew 26:38–39, where Jesus bares his soul before the Father. There is not a thought that Jesus is having that is not brought before the Father. Jesus asked God to take away the circumstances that were closing in on Him. His crucifixion was near. Jesus' soul was "overwhelmed with sorrow to the point of death" (v. 38).

Have you been to this place? I have. I have been to this place many times as I have faced all kinds of heartbreak in my life. My prayer in this place is much like Jesus' prayer. I pray that God will make things better. But no matter what God's answer, I pray that I will have more of Him in my life. I pray that I will learn to depend on Him more fully and that the Potter will use this experience to imprint my life with more of His holiness. I have also been to this place when I've witnessed God do miraculous things in my life. Times where I knew the hand of God paused for a moment and orchestrated a miracle just for me. Oh, how God longs for us to come to this place with Him. How He longs to be intimately acquainted with His beloved children. This should be your most treasured friendship and one that you allow to have the greatest impact on the person you are in the process of becoming.

Level 2: The Inner Circle

The word that characterizes this circle is *interdependence*. These are the people you call on during your hour of need. Jesus had Peter, James, and John, who filled the shoes of those who walked closest with Him. These were the three He asked to come apart from the other disciples and pray for Him. Although they were tired, they were willing to go with Him. These were the friends with whom He shared His deepest thoughts.

We must choose the friends in this circle very carefully and prayerfully. They are the ones who have the greatest ability to guide us and the ones whom we should trust enough to have them hold us accountable. Time with these friends should be a time of renewal, sweet fellowship, and precious encouragement. These are the friends who will go one step further than just cheering us on in this race of life. They are the friends who, when we trip and fall, will jump onto the track, wrap their arms around our shoulders, and support us until we are able to run alone once more.

Level 3: The Influence Circle

The word that characterizes this circle is *impact*. These are the people who are allowed close enough so that we and they mutually influence and impact one another's lives. Jesus' other nine disciples fell into this category. These are friends you are in contact with often and whose advice you value. They are the ones you enjoy being with because you're walking the same path in life—and life's journeys are always much more fun when you are accompanied by such friends. You also have an incredible opportunity for mentoring within this circle. Those younger in life experiences need your advice and encouragement. Those further along in their walk than you can be wonderful mentors in your life.

One important factor to remember about both the inner circle and the influence circle is that these friends should have ongoing and personal relationships with God. Because of their influence in your life, you want to make sure that their advice and guidance comes from a source that can be trusted. Remember: You will be like those whom you allow to be closest, so choose these friends carefully. Look for people whom you enjoy and can trust, people who reflect godly character and have the potential to be a positive influence on you.

Level 4: The Interaction Circle

The word that characterizes this circle is *incarnational ministry*. These are the people you interact with and for whom you have the opportunity to be a physical reminder of the characteristics of Jesus. What an incredible difference Jesus made in the lives of those who interacted with Him. We have the same responsibility.

I think it's so appropriate that Jesus' profession early in life was that of a carpenter. Even after He left His earthly father's shop He continued to be a builder. But instead of fashioning wood, He worked to build into people's lives the love of His heavenly Father. He continues even to this day in His carpentry work, as He promised us when He left that He's gone to prepare a place for us. We should be just as diligent being builders in the lives of those we interact with so that many may see the magnificent place prepared by our Master Carpenter.

Consider the model Jesus gave us for friendships. Maybe you need to find some friends. Pray and ask God to direct you to the right women. Practice being the kind of friend you want to have. Maybe you realize that you have let some of the wrong people get too close and that these people are not being the kind of influence you need. Pray and ask God to help you pull back from these friendships and seek out other persons who can be godly influences in your life. Identify the friends you have that fall within each circle and commit today to developing those relationships and following Jesus' example. Remember: You will become like those with whom you spend the most time, so make sure these people reflect a character worth modeling. George Hubert said it best when he said, "The best mirror is an old friend."

Investing in the Lives of Others

Not only do we need to choose our friends wisely, but we must also be willing to invest ourselves into these relationships. I love the vivid picture painted by King Solomon in Ecclesiastes 4:9–12 of the value of friends:

Two are better than one, because they have a good return for their work: If one falls down, his friend can help him up. But pity the man who falls and has no one to help him up! Also, if two lie down together, they will keep warm. But how can one keep warm alone? Though one may be overpowered, two can defend themselves. A cord of three strands is not quickly broken.

There is comfort, help, warmth, and security in having friends by your side.

I saw this demonstrated so clearly recently when I ran into a bit of trouble along life's highway. I have always been quite daring and eager to take on challenges. That's why transporting a table on top of my minivan was not intimidating to me. There was not enough room to fit the table inside the van, so the only other logical solutions were to rent a U-Haul (too expensive considering the number of miles I needed to travel) or to somehow strap the table onto the luggage rack atop my van (costs nothing—a much better option).

So I climbed up onto a chair, lined the top of my van with a blanket, hoisted the table on top of the van, and secured it with a couple of bungie cords. Everything was going well until I reached the highway and started cruising along at sixty miles per hour. That's when it started. Everyone who passed me made some kind of gesture. Some honked, others waved and pointed to the top of my van, and others tried to communicate in their own rendition of sign language. I was quick to understand that something was wrong with my table.

I pulled over and got out to examine my wooden passenger. It seemed fine. The cords were tight and the table felt secure. As I walked around the van and examined it from every angle, I kept thinking, *What were all those crazy people having such a fit about?* I decided to keep on going. Once again, the people who passed me were having a fit about something. So I pulled over once again. I quickly became annoyed, as everything appeared fine. The table and the cords were in place. I started out once again along the highway and—you guessed it—my problems continued.

Finally, one man did what many others should have done miles back. He pulled alongside me to let me know I had a problem and then was kind enough to pull off the highway with me to offer his assistance. It turned out that when I got going at highway speeds, the air flowing over the top of the van lifted the table up, causing great concern to my fellow drivers. This nice man helped me secure the table in a way that would prevent this from happening and then followed me for the next couple of miles to watch the table and make sure I did not have any further problems.

That's the role of a true friend. To have people who are willing to invest their lives in yours during the good times and the bad. The good times are easy, but it's those times when you've got a wooden table about to fly off the top of your van that you find out who your real friends are.

You see, a real friend will not leave you when trouble strikes. No, a real friend pulls alongside of you, pulls off life's highway with you, helps in any way she can, and then follows close behind to make sure you're all right. That's what it means to invest in the lives of others. It means taking time to give to others as Christ has given to you. It means pulling off the fast track at times to sit and minister to another. It means knowing how to point out inoffensively things that may need attention and when to keep your mouth shut and love unconditionally. A real friend is there for you day or night, when it's convenient or not, and considers it a privilege to help any way she can. And, she knows you'd do the same for her. The best way to *find* this kind of friend is to *be* this kind of friend.

The ABC's of Taming the Tongue

The Bible is full of examples of well-meaning friends threatening their relationships because they could not tame their tongues. We see Job's friends giving bad advice, Jesus' friends betraying Him, and Paul's friends at the church in Ephesus struggling to get rid of words of bitterness, anger, and slander. My mother once remarked that she sure was glad that God only gave us one mouth because one is hard enough to handle. Having had five girls, she should know!

Isn't it interesting that God designed us with two eyes, ears, arms, legs, lungs, kidneys, hands, nostrils, feet, ankles, and shoulders. It would seem that a pair of every part might be the trend. However he only gave us one heart, one mind, and one mouth. In the Bible He cautions us about these singular parts of the body. He warns us that we should be careful not to let our minds be conformed to the pattern of this world (Romans 12:2). He warns us in Jeremiah 17:9 that the heart is deceitful above all things. In James He describes the tongue as the most vicious body part (James 3:1–12). It is as sharp as a sword (Psalm 57:4) and able to break bones (Proverbs 25:15). Do you remember the saying we used to chant when we were children? "Sticks and stones may break my bones but words will never hurt me." Well, I think the rhyme would be much more truthful by saying, "Sticks and stones may break my bones, but words are what will crush me."

Have you ever been crushed by someone's words? I certainly have. There is such power in the tongue. It is responsible for inspiring people to do great things: invent the impossible, win battles against all odds, and proclaim to the multitudes that there is a Father in heaven who loves them. However, for all the potential it has to do good, it also has just as much destructive power. It has brought down kings and kingdoms, destroyed marriages, and to those who used it to reject God, sent them to a damnable eternity. The choice is ours. We can choose to have tongues that inspire, encourage, and please the Lord or ones that destroy others and are detestable to God. Here's an ABC guide for seeking to tame the tongue. These principles are straight from Ephesians 4:29 (NASB), which says, "Let no unwholesome word proceed from your mouth, but only such a word as is good for edification according to the need of the moment, that it may give grace to those who hear."

A—Accentuate the Positive

No matter how negative a situation may seem, there is something positive that can be the focus of your attention. When you accentuate the positive, the negative becomes less and less significant. We must dedicate the words of our mouth to the Lord every day, seek His help through prayer, and guard our words by heeding the advice in His.

B—Build Others Up

Look for opportunities to be an encourager in the lives of those around you. My dear friend and partner with Proverbs 31, Sharon Jaynes, was a writer for nearly fifteen years before any of the words she penned were ever shared with others. One day she took a chance and showed me a couple of stories she had written, and instantly my heart stirred. I encouraged Sharon to pull those precious stories of hers out of the drawer she'd been keeping them in and send them to a publisher. Today she is the author of three books, with many others on the horizon. What dreams could those around you realize with just a little of your encouragement?

C—Concentrate on Giving Out Grace

I think about Jesus living on this earth and dealing with people who grossly distorted God's original design for us as His children. The common thread woven throughout almost all of His encounters with people is grace. Jesus concentrated not on their mistakes, sins, and shortcomings but rather on the grace that forgives, comforts, and heals. To be more like Jesus means to look past a person's humanness into their wounded soul and extend helping hands full of God's transforming grace.

Your Purpose as a Godly Friend

God designed us to need other people. We all have a need for people we can call our friends. Just like athletes need their fans, we need people who will sit in our cheering section and encourage and inspire us, have fun and laugh with us, cry with us, and lend a helping hand during the tough times. Our purpose as godly friends is to do this for those around us whom we have the privilege to call our friends. Again, we must also be willing to let our friends do this for us. We must choose our friends carefully and wisely. We must look for those who are pursuing God and seeking Him with all their heart.

Friends who are prayerful, joyful, and loving are treasures from heaven we should consider some of our greatest blessings. We should look for ways to put our friends before ourselves and help them to become all that they can be. Our friendships should be characterized by openness and trust, so as to foster loving accountability. Above all else, our friendships should be full of Christ's forgiveness, mercy, grace, and love.

WORKING ON YOUR JOURNAL

Take time to work on Section 2, Part 15, of your journal. If you have *The Life Planning Journal for Women,* turn there now. (The questions listed below are already included in the journal itself.) If you are making your own journal, transfer the questions below to your journal and spend some time recording your answers. Then remember to complete each step of the P.U.R.P.O.S.E. model described in chapter 9.

Once you complete this section of your journal, continue your reading with chapter 16, "Reaching Out: Finding My Purpose as a Servant."

QUESTIONS TO CONSIDER IN YOUR JOURNAL

1. Think about the word "friend." Does this word conjure up warm and wonderful thoughts and memories? If yes, journal your thoughts.

2. Does this word sting because of past hurts and rejections? Journal your thoughts.

3. Why do you think Jesus needed friends?

4. Examine the friendship circles model. (Draw the friendship circles just like in the book.)

5. What word characterizes Level 1: "The Intimate Circle"?

   _____

6. Your relationship with God should be your most treasured friendship. How does God know that this is true in your life? What things do you do with God to build your relationship day by day? Journal your thoughts.

7. What word characterizes Level 2: "The Inner Circle"?

   _____

8. Jesus had three friends in this circle. These were the friends with whom He shared His deepest thoughts. Why must we choose the friends in this circle very carefully and prayerfully?

9. Whom do you have in your Inner Circle?

10. Do these friends encourage you in your walk with the Lord? Do they themselves model godly character? Journal your thoughts.

11. Do you need to ask God to send you some friends for your Inner Circle? Is there anyone who is currently in your Inner Circle who perhaps should not be? Journal your prayer.

12. What word characterizes Level 3: "The Influence Circle"?

   _____

13. Jesus' other nine disciples fell into this category. These are the friends who are close enough where you mutually influence and impact each other's lives. Whom do you have in your Influence Circle? What must you remember when choosing these friends?

14. Do you need to ask God for some friends in this circle? Are there some friends in your Influence Circle who are not positive, godly influences on you? Journal your prayer.

15. What word characterizes Level 4: "The Interaction Circle"?
_____.

16. These are the people with whom you have the opportunity to be a physical reminder of the characteristics of Jesus. Whom have you told about Jesus lately?

17. How can you seek to show the love of Christ to those you interact with?

18. Read and record Psalm 57:4.

19. Read and record Proverbs 25:15.

20. What are the ABC's of taming the tongue?

21. Which of these do you do well, and which do you need to work on?

22. What is your purpose as a godly friend? Journal your thoughts.

Chapter Sixteen

REACHING OUT: FINDING MY PURPOSE AS A SERVANT

PRINCIPLE #7: The Proverbs 31 woman shares the love of Christ by extending her hands to help with the needs in her community.

Matthew 11:28–30 says, "Come to me, all you who are weary and burdened, and I will give you rest. Take my yoke upon you and learn from me, for I am gentle and humble in heart, and you will find rest for your souls. For my yoke is easy and my burden is light." By now you may be feeling weary, and wondering—after studying your purpose as a child of God, wife, mother, keeper of the home, faithful steward, and godly friend—how in the world you can possibly muster up the energy to now extend your hand to the community? Well, take heart. God calls all who are weary and burdened to come to Him, and He will give you rest.

How will He give you rest? Because He is fitting you with His yoke. Therefore, you will now find a gentle and humble-in-heart God who delights in His children. He will never give you more than you can handle. Isaiah 43:7 tells us that we were made for His glory. In taking His yoke, you have found your ultimate purpose—to glorify the Father. You see, as you take up the yoke you were made to carry, you will glorify the Father in your obedience to Him. You were never meant to carry the yoke that the world, your parents, your peers, or anyone else tried to place on you. Once you've harnessed yourself to God and the great design He has for you, you will find rest for your soul. This is not an "asleep rest." No, this is a peaceful contentment that you are fit with the right yoke and you are carrying the right load.

Now that you're properly fitted, let's reach out our hands and share the love of Christ. In this chapter we'll talk about carrying our torch into a dark world, dressing ourselves for the battles we'll inevitably face when we are making a difference for Christ, and filling our arms with love. Then we will ponder our purpose as a servant. This is sure to be an exciting chapter, so let's get started.

Carrying the Torch into a Dark World

The Olympic flame has been a time-honored tradition of the Modern Olympic Games since 1928 when a flame was lit and remained burning at the entrance to the Olympic Stadium throughout the Amsterdam Games. The Olympic Torch relay began in 1936 with a flame being lit in Olympia, Greece, and carried to Berlin as a part of the opening ceremonies. This torch relay has remained a part of every Olympic Opening Ceremony since and always begins in Olympia.

I have always enjoyed watching the progression of the Olympic flame leading up to the games almost as much as the games themselves. I sometimes imagine myself as one of these torchbearers when I'm out running. I imagine being surrounded by crowds of people cheering me on as I proudly carry this amazing torch. OK, a bit hokey, I know; however, when you think about this in the spiritual sense, you can draw an amazing correlation to carrying Christ's light into this dark world. Heroes of the faith have gone before us, run the race, and finished victorious, despite hard times and setbacks. Hebrews 12:1 (LB) says, "Since we have such a huge crowd of men of faith watching from the grandstands, let us strip off anything that slows us down or holds us back, and especially those sins that wrap themselves so tightly around our feet and trip us up; and let us run with patience the particular race that God has set before us." God has set a race before us that we are to run, and run victoriously. There is no one that can run it for you. It is your race to run. And you, too, are carrying a torch. It was lit at Calvary, and it beckons to be passed on.

There is a condition we must meet in order to be a qualified torchbearer. We all come to the point at some time in our lives where we have to step past our humanness and into the shadow of the cross. Safety is there. Comfort is there. Redemption is there. Best of all, a Savior with outstretched arms is there—ready, willing, and able to bear your burden and give you peace in exchange. It costs Him everything to be there. It costs you nothing except a willingness to come. Once there, you rest in the warm arms of your heavenly Father, heal, and find a new beginning.

I've been in the shadow of the Cross. I came broken, lost, hurt, and hopeless. I stepped out of the shadow healed and willing to do whatever my heavenly Father asks. Once you've gotten that close to the Cross, you feel compelled to share the transforming love you've found.

After all that I had been through in my life, I thought there was no way God could love me or ever use me. Then one day, in the midst of my brokenness, I stepped close to the cross. Just as He did for Moses the murderer, David the adulterer, Rahab the harlot, and Peter the betrayer, God saw past my flesh and forgave me. He took what the devil meant for evil and used it for His glory. I didn't take God's comfort and stay comfortable. I allowed God to make me comfort-*able,* able to make a difference in the lives of others.

What an amazing thing it has been for me to see God take what was a source of such shame and use it to help others. Yes, my heart still aches for the baby I aborted, but my life is no longer filled with shame. I am forgiven. I know that there are babies alive today because God used my testimony about abortion to change the hearts of those young mothers. I know that there are post-abortive women like myself who thought there was no hope for them. God has allowed me to help them catch a glimpse of Christ's amazing forgiveness, healing power, and love.

Have you been in the shadow of the Cross? Have you felt the touch of the nail-pierced hands? Has His crimson blood washed clean your sin-stained life? It's time now to step across the other side of the shadow. It's time to bask in its light. It's time for the great exchange, where you take the torch carried by the heroes of the faith and carry it on. It's time to run into the darkness of this world and carry His light. It's time to help others move from death to life. It's time to light the path that will lead them into the shadow of the Cross.

Dressing Yourself for the Battle

In reaching out to others with the love of Christ, you will encounter great opposition. Satan will do all he can to discourage and defeat you. When you seek to serve others, you are doing the Father's will. Satan hates those who jump off the fence of complacency and start making a real difference for Christ. You will be on the front lines of the battle and in need of your armor more than ever before. Martin Luther said, "The Bible is alive, it speaks to me; it has feet, it runs after me; it has hands, it lays hold of me." Let the Scriptures from Ephesians 6 come alive as you dress yourself spiritually every day.

The "belt of truth" is to be "buckled around your waist" (Ephesians 6:14). John 8:32 says, "You will know the truth and the truth will set you free." Nothing should bind you but the truth of our Lord. We need to keep our lives free from untruths and secrets. We need to let go of areas in our lives that are sources of shame. The signature of Satan is shame. God does not condemn, He forgives. He died to free you from the chains of sin. Pick up the buckle of truth, fasten it around you, and leave all the chains behind. Let this belt protect you from the lies of Satan.

The "breastplate of righteousness" is for the protection of our hearts (Ephesians 6:14). We need to keep our hearts pure and free from sin. Luke 6:45 says, "The good man brings good things out of the good stored up in his heart, and the evil man brings evil out things of the evil stored up in his heart. For out of the overflow of his heart his mouth speaks." We need to protect what is in our hearts so that the words we speak will honor, not dishonor, the name of the Lord. The only thing we are instructed to store up and hide in our hearts is the word of God (Psalm 119:11). Let this breastplate protect your emotions, safeguard your self-worth, and fend off feelings that are in conflict with your calling.

Our feet should be fitted "with the readiness that comes from the gospel of peace" (Ephesians 6:15). Just as shoes provide protection for our tender "soles," the gospel of peace provides protection for our tender "souls" as we walk the sometimes rocky road in our Christian journey. Our feet can keep us going and moving forward, and they can steady us when we stumble. The gospel gives us that peace so many are searching for but only a few find. We should be eager and ready to share the source of our firm foundation with others. We should let these "holy shoes" protect us as we progress in our Christian walk. We should seek out those who are lost and ask them to join us.

The "shield of faith" protects us from Satan's flaming arrows (Ephesians 6:16). It helps us keep God's perspective when we are hit with hard times, setbacks, insults, and temptations. We can extinguish the enemy's attacks by basing our faith on who God is and not the circumstances we are facing. Hebrews 11:1 says, "Now faith is being sure of what we hope for and certain of what we do not see." Remember to keep the faith. God is who He says He is, and He will do what He has promised.

The "helmet of salvation" is for the protection of our minds (Ephesians 6:17). The enemy wants us to doubt our salvation and the assurance of our future with God. Romans 12:2 says, "Do not conform any longer to the pattern of this world, but be transformed by the renewing of your mind. Then you will be able to test and approve what God's will is—His good, pleasing and perfect will." We can be transformed by renewing our minds with God's Word and spending time with Him. Let us keep the helmet of salvation on to filter out Satan's lies and seeds of doubt.

The "sword of the Spirit" is the last piece of armor and our only offensive weapon (Ephesians 6:17). When Satan tempts us, we must fend him off by quoting God's irrefutable word, just as Jesus did when Satan tried to deflect Him from his glorious mission. We see in Matthew 4, that every temptation Satan threw at Jesus was squelched by the Savior simply by His stating what was written in the Scriptures. Remember, the sword of the Spirit is the true word of God against which the Father of Lies has no defense.

Remember to dress yourself with this spiritual armor daily. It would be foolish to go out in public without your physical clothing, but even more foolish to leave your spiritual armor behind. The battles are real— we must be prepared.

Arms Full of Love

The wives who lived within the walls of the Weinsberg Castle in Germany were well aware of the riches it held: gold, silver, jewels, and wealth beyond belief.

Then the day came in A.D. 1141 when all their treasure was threatened. An enemy army had surrounded the castle and demanded the fortress, the fortune, and the lives of the men within. There was nothing to do but surrender.

Although the conquering commander had set a condition for the safe release of all women and children, the wives of Weinsberg refused to leave without having one of their conditions met, as well. They demanded that they be allowed to fill their arms with as many possessions as they could carry out with them. Knowing that the women couldn't possibly make a dent in the massive fortune, their request was honored.

When the castle gates opened, the army outside was brought to tears. Each woman had carried out her husband.

The wives of Weinsberg, indeed, were well aware of the riches the castle held.[1]

Just like the wives of Weinsberg, we are surrounded by treasure and wealth. Our lives are full of cars, homes, clothes, computers, televisions— and the list goes on and on. I saw a bumper sticker recently that said, "He who dies with the most toys wins." I wanted to chase the car down and tell the driver the truth, but my mini-van just couldn't keep pace with his zippy little sports car. If I could have caught up with him, I would have told him that having the most toys doesn't mean you win, it just means you leave a lot behind. The only things you can carry with you is what can be held in your heart. One day when all the things of this world melt away, we'll look down at our arms and see what we're left holding. Will our arms be full of ash remnants? Or will our arms be filled with treasures of love—lives we have touched, souls we have reached, hungry people we have fed, and naked people we have clothed. In the famous prayer of St. Francis of Assisi, he says, "For it is in the giving that we receive." May we all be willing to extend our hands to touch the lives of those around us just as Jesus would.

Your Purpose as a Servant

In discovering my purpose as a servant, I had to first learn what it meant to serve. I had to understand why Jesus touched the leper, wiped the tear of the adulteress, washed the feet of His disciples, and refused to call down a legion of angels to rescue Him from the cross. He came to serve. He came to give His life. He came to fulfill the Father's purpose.

Am I willing to touch the leper, or do I run for fear of his sores? Am I willing to wipe the tears of the adulteress, or do I draw back a stone-filled fist. Am I willing to wash another's feet, or does my pride keep me from such humble tasks. Am I willing to fulfill the purpose for which I was created, or am I in search of something easier? God, help me to see with Your eyes the needs of those around me. Help be your servant in thought and in deed.

I was hungry and you formed a humanities club to discuss my hunger.
Thank you.

I was imprisoned and you crept off quietly to your chapel to pray for my release.
Nice.

I was naked and in your mind you debated the morality of my appearance.
What good did that do?

I was sick and you knelt and thanked God for your health.
But I needed you.

I was homeless and you preached to me of the shelter of the love of God.
I wish you'd taken me home.

I was lonely and you left me alone to pray for me.

Why didn't you stay?

You seem so holy, so close to God; but I'm still very hungry, lonely, cold, and still in pain.

Does it matter?

Anonymous

WORKING ON YOUR JOURNAL

Take time to work on Section 2, Part 16, of your journal. If you have *The Life Planning Journal for Women,* turn there now. (The questions listed below are already included in the journal itself.) If you are making your own journal, transfer the questions below to your journal and spend some time recording your answers. Then remember to complete each step of the P.U.R.P.O.S.E. model described in chapter 9.

Once you complete this section of your journal, continue your reading with chapter 17, "Let God Do Amazing Things with Your Life."

QUESTIONS TO CONSIDER IN YOUR JOURNAL

1. Read Matthew 11:28-30. Journal your thoughts about this verse.
2. Read and record Isaiah 43:7. According to this verse, what is your ultimate purpose?
3. Have you ever tried to carry a yoke put on you by anyone but God? Journal your thoughts.
4. What torch are you to carry in this race of life?
5. What do you need to do to be a qualified torchbearer? Journal your thoughts.
6. Have you been in the shadow of the cross?
7. Have you felt the touch of the nail-pierced hands?
8. Has His crimson blood washed clean your sin-stained life?
9. It's time to carry the torch. Are you willing?

10. What battles will you face because you are touching others for Christ?

11. How can you dress yourself for battle? List your spiritual armor and what each piece protects.

12. How did the story about the wives of Weinsberg touch your heart? Journal your thoughts.

13. Are you willing to fulfill your purpose as a servant? Journal a prayer to God.

Note

1. This story, "For Richer or Poorer," is retold by Rochelle M. Pennington, newspaper columnist and contributing author to *Stories for the Heart, Chicken Soup for the Soul,* and *Life's Little Instruction Book,* and co-author of *Highlighted in Yellow.* You may reach her at N3535 Corpus Christi Circle, Campbellsport, WI 53010; (920) 533-5880. Used by permission.

Chapter Seventeen

LET GOD DO AMAZING THINGS WITH YOUR LIFE

What word comes to mind when you hear the name Alfred Nobel? For most people it would be the word "peace" because of the famous Nobel Peace Prize. I once read an interesting and sobering story about Mr. Nobel. When his brother died, Nobel obtained a newspaper to read what the obituary said. Much to his dismay, he discovered that the paper had made a terrible error and printed an obituary about Alfred instead of his late brother. He was reading his own obituary and he did not like what was written. The paper told of his involvement with the invention of dynamite and went on to elaborate on the terrible death and destruction this powerful substance had brought into the world. Ken Blanchard, in *The Heart of a Leader,* recounts Nobel's reaction to his obituary. "Nobel was devastated. He wanted to be known as a man of 'peace.' He quickly realized that if his obituary was to be rewritten, he would have to do it himself by changing the nature of his life. So Alfred Nobel did just that. I dare say that Alfred Nobel is better known today for his contribution to peace than for any other thing he did in his life."[1]

What do you want to be known as? When your descendants talk of you and your contribution to your family and to the world, what will they have to say? What will be the major theme of your life? If you were to have the chance that Alfred Nobel had to read your obituary before your death, would you like what it said? I would have had no idea how to answer these questions ten years ago. I had no idea what I stood for and had given my purpose little thought. Today, however, I can answer the tough fundamental questions of life, and even more than that, I have a plan to help me live every area of my life on purpose. Having a Life Plan has completely changed my life. Do you remember the story I shared with you at the beginning of this book? Well, life is a lot different now. Instead of waking up feeling overwhelmed and frustrated, I wake up with an excited expectancy concerning all that my days hold. I actually enjoy following a schedule and have seen the most amazing results from setting goals and scheduling time to complete the necessary action steps. The book you are holding in your hands proves that God is still in the miracle business. If He could transform this planning-challenged gal to the point where she could write a book on the subject, trust me, He can do amazing things in your life.

That's my prayer for you. I want you to be willing to let God do amazing things with your life. I hope that by reading this book you have laughed and identified with the comedy of errors I've shared. I also hope your heart has been stirred to action as I've recounted how God can transform a person through a Life Plan. I pray you now have a clear understanding of the incredible purpose for which you were created and a clear vision of where you are headed from here. I also pray that your Life Plan will be an invaluable tool you can use, add to, revise, and update.

I am so excited that we have taken this Life Planning journey together. I hope you have discovered amazing things about God, yourself, and the incredible impact you can have as a woman of purpose. If there is just one thought I might leave you with, it is this: God values you and the purpose for which He created you. There are no insignificant people or small purposes. After all, the God of the universe, the one who formed the earth, set the stars and the sun in place, established the heavens, and made every living creature great and small, created you for such a time as this.

You are the only person who can fulfill the purpose for which God created you. You are the woman God created to be your husband's help-mate. You have the incredible opportunity to be the mother of your children. You are needed in your home to be its safe keeper. You have been entrusted with time and resources and will be held accountable to be a faithful steward. You are a special woman who needs friends and is needed by others for your love, support, and encouragement. And finally, you are surrounded by a community of people who need to see Jesus through you. In light of all of this, isn't your life worth living on purpose? I think so and even more importantly, God thinks so.

WORKING ON YOUR JOURNAL

Take time to work on Section 2, Part 17, of your journal. If you have *The Life Planning Journal for Women,* turn there now. If you are writing out your own journal, write out a letter of commitment to let God do amazing things with your life. As you write this letter, incorporate things you have learned throughout this study. Be sure to include ways your heart has been encouraged, your mind challenged, and your walk with the Lord strengthened.

Dear Reader,

Thank you for taking time to read and study *Living Life on Purpose.* I thought it might be helpful for you to have a format for a Bible study, should you chose to take this wonderful journey in a group setting. If you are considering leading this Bible study and would like to purchase my one hour seminar tape to use with your group, please contact The Proverbs 31 Ministry toll-free at 1(877) 731-4663, and request the *Living Life on Purpose* cassette tape.

God Bless,

Lysa TerKeurst

GROUP BIBLE STUDY FORMAT

For use with Living Life on Purpose and *The Life Planning Journal for Women*
A Twelve-Week Format

Week One:
   Book: Read the Introduction and chapters 1 and 2
   Journal: Complete Section 1, Part 1 and 2

Week Two:
   Book: Read chapters 3 and 4
   Journal: Complete Section 1, Parts 3 and 4

Week Three:
   Book: Read chapters 5 and 6
   Journal: Complete Section 1, Parts 5 and 6

Week Four:
   Book: Read chapters 7 and 8
   Journal: Complete Section 1, Parts 7 and 8

Week Five:
    Book: Read chapters 9 and 10
    Journal: Complete Section 2, Parts 9 and 10

Week Six:
    Book: Read chapter 11
    Journal: Complete Section 2, Part 11

Week Seven:
    Book: Read chapter 12
    Journal: Complete Section 2, Part 12

Week Eight:
    Book: Read chapter 13
    Journal: Complete Section 2, Part 13

Week Nine:
    Book: Read chapter 14
    Journal: Complete Section 2, Part 14

Week Ten:
    Book: Read chapter 15
    Journal: Complete Section 2, Part 15

Week Eleven:
    Book: Read chapter 16
    Journal: Complete Section 2, Part 16

Week Twelve:
    Book: Read chapter 17
    Journal: Complete Section 2, Part 17. Use the group time to share
       with one another how this study has changed your life.

I would love to hear your testimonies of how God has worked in your life through this study.

Please send them to:
The Proverbs 31 Ministry
Attn: Lysa TerKeurst
PO Box 17155
Charlotte, NC 28227

NOTE

1. Ken Blanchard, *The Heart of a Leader* (Tulsa: Honor, 1999), 157.

Appendix A

SETTING UP YOUR OWN LIFE PLANNING JOURNAL

*I*f you did not purchase *The Life Planning Journal for Women* with this book, you will want to purchase a three-ring binder and label your sections as follows:

Setting Up Your Own Journal
Section 1: Understanding the Fundamental Questions of Life

Part 1—What Will a Life Plan Do for Me?
   • Answer the questions from chapter 1 in the book.

Part 2—The Fundamentals of a Life Plan
   • Answer the questions from chapter 2 in the book.

Part 3—My Foundation: "Who am I?"
* Answer the questions from chapter 3 in the book.
* Write your Foundation Statement.

Part 4—My Purpose: "Why Do I Exist?"
* Answer the questions from chapter 4 in the book.
* Write your Purpose Statement.

Part 5—My Mission: "What Am I to Do?"
* Answer the questions from chapter 5 in the book.
* Write your Mission Statement.

Part 6—My Ministry: "Where Am I to Serve?"
* Answer the questions from chapter 6 in the book.
* Write your Ministry Statement.

Part 7—My Stages of Life: "When Am I to Do These Things?"
* Answer the questions from chapter 7 in the book.
* Write your Stage of Life Statement.

Part 8—My Principles: "How Am I to Live my Day-to-Day Life?"
* Answer the questions from chapter 8 in the book.
* Write out the Seven Principles of the Proverbs 31 Woman.

Section 2: Living Every Area of My Life on Purpose

Part 9—Finding P.U.R.P.O.S.E. in Each of My Principles
* Answer the questions from chapter 9 in the book.

Part 10—The Holy Pursuit: Finding My Purpose as a Child of God
* Answer the questions from chapter 10 in the book.
* Follow the P.U.R.P.O.S.E. model (as described in chapter 9) for writing this part of your Life Plan.

P—Pray

U—Understand God's Word

R—Record Key Scriptures

P—Plan Your Goals

O—Outline Your Action Steps

S—Set a Realistic Schedule

E—Examine Your Progress

Part 11—Making the Most of My Marriage: Finding My Purpose as a Wife
- Answer the questions from chapter 11 in the book.
- Follow the P.U.R.P.O.S.E. model (as described in chapter 9) for writing this part of your Life Plan.

P —Pray

U—Understand God's Word

R—Record Key Scriptures

P —Plan Your Goals

O—Outline Your Action Steps

S —Set a Realistic Schedule

E —Examine Your Progress

Part 12—The High Calling of Motherhood: Finding My Purpose as a Mother
- Answer the questions from chapter 12 in the book.
- Follow the P.U.R.P.O.S.E. model (as described in chapter 9) for writing this part of your Life Plan.

P —Pray

U—Understand God's Word

R—Record Key Scriptures

P —Plan Your Goals

O—Outline Your Action Steps

S —Set a Realistic Schedule

E —Examine Your Progress

Part 13—There's No Place Like Home: Finding My Purpose as
a Keeper of the Home
- Answer the questions from chapter 13 in the book.
- Follow the P.U.R.P.O.S.E. model (as described in chapter 9) for writing this part of your Life Plan.

P —Pray
U—Understand God's Word
R—Record Key Scriptures
P —Plan Your Goals
O—Outline Your Action Steps
S —Set a Realistic Schedule
E —Examine Your Progress

Part 14—Time and Money: Finding My Purpose as a Faithful
Steward
- Answer the questions from chapter 14 in the book.
- Follow the P.U.R.P.O.S.E. model (as described in chapter 9) for writing this part of your Life Plan.

P —Pray
U—Understand God's Word
R—Record Key Scriptures
P —Plan Your Goals
O—Outline Your Action Steps
S —Set a Realistic Schedule
E —Examine Your Progress

Part 15—The Gift of Godly Friendships: Finding My Purpose
as a Godly Friend
- Answer the questions from chapter 15 in the book.
- Follow the P.U.R.P.O.S.E. model (as described in chapter 9) for writing this part of your Life Plan.

P —Pray
U—Understand God's Word

R—Record Key Scriptures
P —Plan Your Goals
O—Outline Your Action Steps
S —Set a Realistic Schedule
E —Examine Your Progress

Part 16—Reaching Out: Finding My Purpose as a Servant
    • Answer the questions from chapter 16 in the book.
    • Follow the P.U.R.P.O.S.E. model (as described in chapter 9) for writing this part of your Life Plan.

P —Pray
U—Understand God's Word
R—Record Key Scriptures
P —Plan Your Goals
O—Outline Your Action Steps
S —Set a Realistic Schedule
E —Examine Your Progress

Part 17—Let God Do Amazing Things with Your Life
    • Write your letter of commitment as described in chapter 17 of the book.

When it is time to write in your journal, you will find it helpful to refer back to chapter 9, "Finding P.U.R.P.O.S.E. in Each of My Principles," for direction on completing each part within chapters 10–16. You will also find it helpful to transfer the questions at the end of each chapter into the appropriate sections of your journal.

Appendix B

DEFINITIONS OF THE DIFFERENT SPIRITUAL GIFTS

Preaching ("Prophecy"): 1 Corinthians 14:3: The ability to publicly communicate God's Word in an inspired way that convinces unbelievers and both challenges and comforts believers. The ability to persuasively declare God's will.

Evangelism: Acts 8:26–40: The ability to communicate the Good News of Jesus Christ to unbelievers in a positive, non-threatening way. The ability to sense opportunities to share Christ and lead people to respond with faith.

Missions: 1 Corinthians 9:19–23; Acts 13:2–3: The ability to adapt to a culture in order to reach unbelievers and help believers from that culture.

Apostle: Romans 15:20: The ability to start new churches and oversee their development.

Teaching: Ephesians 4:12–13: The ability to educate God's people by clearly explaining and applying the Bible in a way that causes them to learn. The ability to equip and train other believers for ministry.

Encouragement ("Exhortation"): Acts 14:22: The ability to motivate God's people to apply and act on biblical principles, especially when they are discouraged or wavering in their faith. The ability to bring out the best in others and challenge them to develop their potential.

Wisdom: 1 Corinthians 2:1, 6–16: The ability to understand God's perspective on life situations and share those insights in a simple, understandable way. The ability to explain what to do and how to do it.

Discernment: 1 John 4:1–6: The ability to distinguish right from wrong, truth from error, and to give an immediate evaluation based on God's Word. The ability to discern whether the source of an experience is Satan, self, or God's Spirit.

Knowledge: Daniel 1:17: The ability to discover, collect, analyze, and organize information that is vital to individual believers or the entire church family. The ability to comprehend a large amount of information and provide it when needed for effective decision making.

Service: Acts 6:1–7: The ability to recognize unmet needs in the church family, and take the initiative to provide practical assistance quickly, cheerfully, and without a need for recognition.

Mercy: Luke 10:30–37: The ability to detect hurt and empathize with those who are suffering in the church family. The ability to provide compassionate and cheerful support to those experiencing distress, crisis, or pain.

Hospitality: 1 Peter 4:9–10: The ability to make others, especially strangers, feel warmly welcome, accepted, and comfortable in the church family. The ability to coordinate factors that promote fellowship.

Pastoring ("Shepherding"): 1 Peter 5:2–4: The ability to care for the spiritual needs of a group of believers and equip them for ministry. The ability to nurture a small group in spiritual growth and assume responsibility for their welfare.

Giving: 2 Corinthians 8:1–7: The ability to generously contribute material resources and/or money beyond the 10 percent tithe so that the body of Christ may grow and be strengthened. The ability to earn and manage money so it may be given to support the ministry of others.

Music: Psalm 150: The ability to celebrate God's presence through music, either vocal or instrumental, and lead the church family in worship.

Arts and Crafts: Exodus 31:3–11: The ability to build, maintain, or beautify the place of worship for God's glory. The ability to express worship through a variety of art forms.

Intercession: Colossians 1:9–12: The ability to pray for the needs of others in the church family over extended periods of time on a regular basis. The ability to persist in prayer and not be discouraged until the answer arrives.

Healing: James 5:13–16: The ability to pray in faith specifically for people who need physical, emotional, or spiritual healing and see God answer. The ability to sense when God is prompting you to pray this kind of prayer.

Miracles: Mark 11:23–24: The ability to pray in faith specifically for God's supernatural intervention into an impossible situation and see God answer. The ability to sense when God is prompting you to pray this kind of prayer.

Praying with My Spirit (Tongues/Interpretation): 1 Corinthians 14:13–15: The ability to pray in a language understood only by God or one who is given the gift of interpretation at that time.

Leadership: Hebrews 13:7, 17: The ability to clarify and communicate the purpose and direction ("Vision") of a ministry in a way that attracts others to get involved. The ability to motivate others by example to work together in accomplishing a ministry goal.

Administration ("Organization"): 1 Corinthians 14:40: The ability to recognize the gifts of others and recruit them to a ministry. The ability to organize and manage people, resources, and time for effective ministry. The ability to coordinate many details and execute the plans of leadership.

Faith: Romans 4:18–21: The ability to trust God for what cannot be seen and to act on God's promise, regardless of what the circumstances indicate. The willingness to risk failure in pursuit of a God-given vision, expecting God to handle the obstacles.

———

This list of Spiritual Gifts is used by permission of Pastor Rick Warren from his Discovering My Ministry Class #301, which he teaches at Saddleback Community Church in California. You can find more information about the resources available from Rick Warren through reviewing the Web site www.pastors.com.

For further study on Spiritual Gifts, you may be interested in the following resources:

Leslie Flynn. *The Nineteen Gifts of the Spirit: Which Do You Have? Are You Using Them?* Colorado Springs: Chariot Victor, 1999.

Charles R. Swindoll. *He Gave Gifts.* Tape Series and Study Guide. Anaheim, Calif.: Insight for Living, 1998. (Available at your local bookstore, or can be ordered through Insight for Living, 1-800-772-8888.)

Charles Peter Wagner. *Your Spiritual Gifts Can Help Your Church Grow.* Ventura, Calif.: Regal, 1979, 1982.

Appendix C

MY FUNDAMENTAL LIFE STATEMENTS AND THE SEVEN PRINCIPLES OF THE PROVERBS 31 WOMAN

My Fundamental Life Statements

My Foundation: I am a child of God. This is who I am. My relationship with Jesus Christ is not merely the religion compartment of my life but rather the foundation that everything else in my life is built on and around. My identity is solid. God calls me a holy and dearly loved child who is adopted as one of His very own. Because of this, I should never question my self-worth. God sent His only son to die on a cross to save me from my sin so that I could spend eternity with Him. There is purpose to my existence, value in the mission I am to accomplish, a ministry that needs my service, and seasons of life to be enjoyed. I am committed to live by my seven basic principles, so that I can be all that God intended for me to be. My life is a gift from God. Living a life that honors God and draws others to know and love Him, is my gift back.

My Purpose: My purpose for existing is to be in constant fellowship with Jesus so he can shape and mold me to be like Himself. In my day-to-day life, I desire to seek God as I live intentionally and make the most of every opportunity that He gives me. I believe I was created to be used as a vessel through which God can encourage and equip others to become all that He intended for them to be. I have been blessed with special abilities to write and speak. I feel passionate about using my gifts of evangelism, teaching, and wisdom to be a woman of godly influence in the lives of my husband, my children, and others whom I touch.

My Mission: In my role as a servant of Christ, I have been called to be a transparent person who is willing to share my life experiences, both good and bad, and to live a victorious Christian life that draws others to Christ. As a wife, I have been called to be my husband's helpmate and complete him so that he can be the man God wants him to be. As a mother, I have been called to be a Christlike example to my daughters while instilling in them strong character, biblical values, and the desire to follow Christ. As a friend, I am called to love and give of myself to make life a sweeter experience for those I touch.

My Ministry: I am fulfilling my purpose and answering the call of my mission by serving in my home, my church, and through the Proverbs 31 Ministry. I am making my home a safe haven where my family can find a loving wife and mother who meets their physical and emotional needs. At church, I serve where I am gifted (in evangelism and teaching) and where I am needed (in the children's ministry). Through the Proverbs 31 Ministry, I am touching women's hearts and helping them to build godly homes through my writing, speaking at conferences and on the radio, and by serving in the leadership of the ministry.

My Stage of Life: I am a wife and mother of three young daughters. My schedule is hectic at times because of the physical needs of my family, but tremendously exciting. As I am learning to serve and meet the needs of my husband, God is teaching me the value of submission, the rewards of a servant attitude, and how wonderful love is when He is at the center of a relationship. Through my experiences as a parent, God has allowed me to more clearly understand His love for me. He loves me even more than I love my children. Therefore, He must discipline and teach me just as I discipline and teach my daughters. At this stage of my life, I must make a conscious effort to make the most of every minute so that I will be able to balance the demands of ministry while giving my family all that they deserve from me. In order to manage my time effectively, I must schedule my time according to my priorities.

THE SEVEN PRINCIPLES OF THE PROVERBS 31 WOMAN

1. The Proverbs 31 woman reveres Jesus Christ as Lord of her life and pursues an ongoing personal relationship with Him.

2. The Proverbs 31 woman loves, honors and respects her husband as head of the home.

3. The Proverbs 31 woman nurtures her children and believes that motherhood is a high calling with the responsibility of shaping and molding the children who will one day define who we are as a community and nation.

4. The Proverbs 31 woman is a disciplined and industrious keeper of the home who creates a warm and loving environment for her family and friends.

5. The Proverbs 31 woman contributes to the financial wellbeing of her household by being a faithful steward of the time and money God has entrusted to her.

6. The Proverbs 31 woman speaks with wisdom and faithful instruction as she mentors and supports other women and develops godly friendships.

7. The Proverbs 31 woman shares the love of Christ by extending her hands to help with the needs in her community.

About The Proverbs 31 Ministry

The **Proverbs 31 Ministry** is a non-denominational organization dedicated to glorifying God by touching women's hearts to build godly homes. Through Jesus Christ, we shed light on God's distinctive design for women and the great responsibilities we have been given. With Proverbs 31:10-31 as a guide, we encourage and equip women to practice living out their faith as wives, mothers, friends and neighbors.

What began in 1992 as a monthly newsletter has now grown into a multi-faceted ministry reaching women across the country and around the globe. Each aspect of the ministry seeks to equip women in the Seven Principles of the **Proverbs 31 Woman**.

1. The Proverbs 31 woman reveres Jesus Christ as Lord of her life and pursues an ongoing, personal relationship with Him.

2. The Proverbs 31 woman loves, honors, and respects her husband as the leader of the home.

3. The Proverbs 31 woman nurtures her children and believes that motherhood is a high calling with the responsibility of shaping and molding the children who will one day define who we are as a community and a nation.

4. The Proverbs 31 woman is a disciplined and industrious keeper of the home who creates a warm and loving environment for her family and friends.

5. The Proverbs 31 woman contributes to the financial well-being of her household by being a faithful steward of the time and money God has entrusted to her.

6. The Proverbs 31 woman speaks with wisdom and faithful instruction as she mentors and supports other women, and develops godly friendships.

7. The Proverbs 31 woman shares the love of Christ by extending her hands to help with the needs in the community.

Ministry Features

Newsletter: The Proverbs 31 Woman is a twelve-page, monthly publication which is a storehouse of inspiration and information to equip women in the seven principles of the Proverbs 31 woman.

Radio Ministry: The Proverbs 31 Radio Ministry airs a daily two-minute program heard on approximately 400 networks across the country and overseas.

Speaking Ministry: The Proverbs 31 Ministry features dynamic speakers who share life-changing and inspirational messages at women's conferences, banquets, and retreats.

On-line Support Group: Through the Internet, this support group includes an on-line Bible study and book club for women who may not otherwise have an opportunity for fellowship.

For a sample issue of our newsletter, or more information on the ministry, write or call:

The Proverbs 31 Ministry
PO Box 17155
Charlotte, NC 28227
877-p31-home (877-731-4663)
web site: www.proverbs31.org

More Excellent Resources from The Proverbs 31 Ministry

The Life Planning Journal for Woman

0-8024-4196-3
Quality Paperback

The Life Planning Journal for Women is an excellent companion to help women apply the life-changing principles found in *Living Life on Purpose*. This unique journal will help women achieve their goals, stay faithful to their appointed action steps, and fulfill their plan for living their lives on purpose. Each chapter is broken into a devotional on the principle, journal space, and concrete action steps for women to apply the principle to their lives.

Being a Great Mom, Raising Great Kids

0-8024-6531-5
Quality Paperback

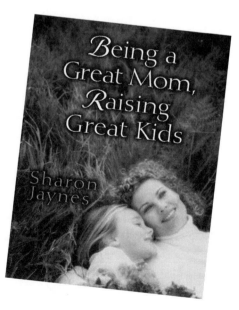

Mothers today are so harried and over-committed that their priorities are all out of whack. What they need is to be refreshed by God's vision for motherhood. Sharon Jaynes, President of The Proverbs 31 Ministry, offers women the opportunity to be encouraged that motherhood is a high and holy calling of Almighty God. She methodically teaches women how to focus on becoming the mother of the Proverbs 31 whose children will one day rise up and bless her. Through the creative and handy use of the acronym B.L.E.S.S.E.D., Sharon provides mothers the practical suggestions and loving encouragement that is surely needed.

Lysa TerKeurst is available
for speaking engagements. For more
information on this or the Proverbs
31 Ministry, call toll free:
1-877-P31HOME
(1-877-731-4663)

Moody Press, a ministry of Moody Bible Institute,
is designed for education, evangelization, and edification.
If we may assist you in knowing more about Christ
and the Christian life, please write us without obligation:
Moody Press, c/o MLM, Chicago, Illinois 60610.